WHITE SERVITUDE IN THE COLONY OF VIRGINIA

A STUDY OF THE SYSTEM OF INDENTURED LABOR IN THE AMERICAN COLONIES

By James Curtis Ballagh, A.B.

I0151711

HERITAGE BOOKS
2009

White Servitude in the Colony of Virginia

A STUDY OF THE SYSTEM OF INDENTURED LABOR IN THE AMERICAN COLONIES

By James Curtis Ballagh, A.B.

HERITAGE BOOKS
AN IMPRINT OF HERITAGE BOOKS, INC.

Books, CDs, and more—Worldwide

For our listing of thousands of titles see our website
at
www.HeritageBooks.com

A Facsimile Reprint
Published 2009 by
HERITAGE BOOKS, INC.
Publishing Division
100 Railroad Ave. #104
Westminster, Maryland 21157

Originally Published by
Burt Franklin
235 East 44th Street
New York, New York 10017
1895

International Standard Book Numbers
Paperbound: 978-0-7884-1707-8
Clothbound: 978-0-7884-8089-8

CONTENTS.

SOURCES.

The materials upon which this study is based are largely contained in:

I. The Records of the Virginia Company of London, of which two MS. copies are extant:

(a) The Collingwood MS. (1619-1624), 2 v. folio, Library of Congress, Washington, D. C., prepared for the Earl of Southampton from the original records of the Company, now lost, in 1624, and compared with them page by page by the secretary, Edward Collingwood, and attested by his signature. Through the copious abstracts by the late Conway Robinson, Stith's History of Virginia and the publications of the Rev. E. D. Neill, this MS. is largely accessible in print.

(b) The Randolph MS., formerly the property of John Randolph of Roanoke, now in the library of the Virginia Historical Society, Richmond, 2 v. folio, an 18th century transcript of the Collingwood MS.; and 1 v. folio of miscellaneous correspondence, orders, instructions, etc. (1617—).

II. Documents, correspondence, orders, instructions, proclamations, laws by the Company, Governors' commissions, etc., 1587-1730, to be found in Purchas, Hakluyt, Force, Brown's Genesis of the United States (1605-1616), Smith's works (1606-1624), Calendars of English State Papers (Colonial, East Indies, Domestic, 1578-1676), Jefferson MSS. (1606-1711), MacDonald, De Jarnette, Sainsbury and Winder collections (Virgina MSS. from the British Record Office, 20 v. folio, 1587-1730), Colonial Records of Virginia (1619-1680), Land Books (1621—), and reprints of valuable early papers in the Virginia Historical Register and the Virginia Historical Magazine.

III. (a) The Records of the General Court of Virginia (1670-76), the Robinson MS. (1633—), containing valuable abstracts from the General Court records and other papers since destroyed, the MS. Letters of Wm. Fitzhugh (1679-1699), the MS. Letters of Wm. Byrd (1683-1691), and the Virginia Gazettes (1737—), all in the possession of the Virginia Historical Society.

(b) The MS. County Records of Accomac (1632—), York (1633-1709), Essex (1683-86), Henrico (1686-99), State Library, Richmond, Virginia.

(c) Hening, Statutes at Large of Virginia (1623-1792), and contemporary descriptions of Virginia; Whitaker (1613), Hamor (1614), Rolf (1616), " A Declaration," etc. (1620), Bullock (1649), Williams (1650), Hammond (1656), Blair, Chilton and Hartwell (1696), Beverley (1705), Jones (1724).

Such other authorities as have been referred to will appear in the appended bibliography.

I desire to express my thanks to Philip A. Bruce, Esq., of the Virginia Historical Society; to Messrs. W. W. Scott and W. G. Stanard, of the Virginia State Library; to Col. R. A. Brock, of the Southern Historical Society, and to Hon. A. R. Spofford, Librarian of Congress, for their courtesy in rendering these authorities accessible to me; also to Professors Adams, Emmott and Vincent, of the Johns Hopkins University, for valuable suggestions.

J. C. B.

INTRODUCTION.

The chief interest in the colonial history of America has always centered in the development of political institutions, which, from their importance and endurance, have become of wide significance. For this reason it has been customary to overlook, or to treat as processes subsidiary to the political evolution, many interesting social and economic developments, which were of great moment in the history of the colonial period as furnishing the material background of this political development and giving it its distinctive character.

In this paper an attempt has been made to trace the growth and significance of one such social institution as a result of the peculiar conditions under which the actual colonization took place. Though the study is limited to the experience of a single colony, that experience becomes, through the exceptional position occupied by that colony, broadly characteristic of the institution in general, and in all important particulars typical of the legal form which servitude assumed in the other colonies.

The main ideas on which servitude was based originated in the early history of Virginia as a purely English colonial development before the other colonies were formed. The system was adopted in them with its outline already defined, requiring only local legislation to give it specific character in each colony. Such legislation was in some cases directly copied from the experience of Virginia, and when of independent or prior origin was largely determined by conditions more or less common to all the colonies, so that in its general legal character the institution was much the same in all. The similarity was more striking, both in theory and in practice, in the agricultural colonies of Virginia, Maryland and Pennsylvania, and particularly in them was it of industrial importance.

The conditions in the other middle colonies, New England, the Carolinas and Georgia, were somewhat different and not so favorable to the existence of such an institution. It consequently neither reached so full a development nor continued to exist so long, but while it did it was of considerable social and economic importance, and its effects, though not so marked, were much the same.

The object of the present paper, then, is to show:

First, the purely colonial development of an institution which both legally and socially was distinct from the institution of slavery, which grew up independently by its side, though the two institutions mutually affected and modified each other to some degree.

Second, that it proved an important factor in the social and economic development of the colonies, and conferred a great benefit on England and other portions of Europe in offering a partial solution of their problem of the unemployed.

WHITE SERVITUDE IN THE COLONY OF VIRGINIA.

CHAPTER I.

SERVITUDE UNDER THE LONDON COMPANY.

The failure of individual enterprise to establish a permanent colony in America, and the example of successful commercial corporations, led to an adoption in England of the corporate principle in regard to colonization as well as to trade. The Virginia Company of London, created by letters patent from King James I., April 10, 1606, was organized as a joint stock company on the general plan of such commercial corporations, and particularly on that of the East India Company. The two Companies had the same Governor. The distinction between them lay in the fact that the avowed object of the Virginia Company was to establish a colony of which trade was to be a result, while the India Company aimed at trade alone, and the colonization which resulted was merely incidental.[1]

Though the Virginia Company was composed of two separate divisions, the London Company and the Plymouth Company, the former, which alone effected a permanent colonization, is of interest to us. The charter members of this Company were largely merchants of London, and after its organization was perfected two classes of membership were distinguished: first, "Adventurers," who remained in Eng-

---

[1] Stephens. p. viii.; Bruce, I., 112, 136, 138, 154, 165; S. P. E. I., 10, 215; Cunningham, Growth of English Industry and Commerce, p. 268, cf. 125, 151, 267. Charter of 1606, Brown, p. 72. The peculiar feature of a Royal Council for the government of the Virginia Company was a result of this distinction.

land and subscribed money towards a capital stock; and,
second, "Planters," who went in person as colonists, and
were expected by their industry or trade to greatly enlarge
the stock and its profits. Shares of adventure were granted
for each subscription of £12 10s. to the stock, and also for
each "adventure of the person," entitling the holder to par-
ticipate proportionately to his shares in all divisions of
profits, both those resulting from the industry of the colonists and those resulting from trade, and besides this to
receive a land grant of some nature for each share. A community of property and of trade was to be established in the
colony for five years after the first landing of the colonists,
and at the end of that time doubtless a division of profits
and of land was promised.[1]

---

[1] Nova Britannia, Force, I., 24, 28; Brown, Genesis of the U.
S., I., 228, 229; Charter of 1609; Va. Mag. of Hist. and Biog.,
Oct., 1894, Vol. II., 156, 7, Instructions to Yeardley: Decl. of
Anct. Planters, Col. Rec. Va., 81. We have nothing extant to
show the exact terms on which the colonists of 1606-7 as a
whole, and the "supplies" until 1609, came to Virginia. When
we come to the latter year we have in a pamphlet (Nova
Britannia) and in a "broadside" of the Company, both issued
to attract new adventurers and planters, a perfect .outline of
the Company's policy at that time. There is nothing, however,
so far as I have been able to discover, that contradicts the
view that the outline as we have it for 1609 was in its general
character that of 1606, the chief difference being the length
of the term. which was probably five years in 1606 instead
of the seven years of 1609; on the contrary, all the evidence
we have goes to substantiate this theory. In 1618, the instructions to Yeardley ordered that 100 acres of land be granted
to *each share* owned by every planter, whether sent by the
Company or transferred at his own charge before *the coming
away of Dale* in 1616. This included some of the colonists of
1607. The patent of 1606 specially authorizes the council of
the colony to pass lands, declaring all lands passed "by letters
patent shall be sufficient assurance from the said patentees, so
divided amongst the undertakers for the plantations of the
said several colonies," and shows that a division of land was
contemplated. (Brown, I., 63.) This is established by the fact of
Ancient Planters of 1607 receiving in later years grants of
lands for their personal adventure, and also for subscriptions
to stock. Captain Gabriel Archer's brother inherited one grant

This so-called communal system was provided for in his Majesty's instructions issued a short time after the granting of the patent to the Company. They were to " trade together all in one stocke or devideably, but in two or three stocks at most and bring not only all the fruits of their labours there, but also all such other goods and commodities which shall be brought out of England or any other place into several magazines or store-houses," and " every person of the said several colonies " was to " be furnished with all necessaries out of those several magazines or store-houses for and during the term of five years." An officer called the treasurer or " cape merchant " was to administer this magazine in connection with the President and Council, accounting for all goods taken into and withdrawn from this joint stock.[1]

The position of an early planter was thus theoretically that of a member of the Company, who was to receive in lieu of his service for a term of years his maintenance during that time, or his transportation and maintenance, at the Company's charge. For the adventure of his person, as well as for every subscription of £12 10s., he received a bill of adventure which entitled him to the proportion that

of land from him, and Anthony Gosnold, in 1621, received a share for personal adventure sixteen years before at his own charge. Cf, Brown, II., 814; Neil, Va. Co., 257; Arber's Smith, 390; Burke, Vol. II., 332, 333, 334, under names Dodds, Simons, Martin. It is not to be supposed that mere adventure or gold-seeking would have constituted a sufficient motive to induce many persons to make such an experiment. A land grant of some kind was undoubtedly promised before 1609 in addition to the proportional share of profits. This was in accordance with the policy under which earlier attempts at discovery or colonization had been made. Gilbert's Articles of Agreement with the Merchants Adventurers in 1582, under his patent of 1578, show the same general principle of Adventurers of the purse or person and of land grants, and Carlyle's project presents a scheme of " Adventurers " and " Enterprisers " who are to share equally in the lands, &c., discovered. Sainsbury MS., I., 32, 35; Haklyut, III., 234, 235; Va. Hist. Mag.. Oct. '94, 186.

[1] Brown, I., 71, 72. Instructions, Nov. 20, 1606.

would fall to a single share in a division of land and profits. As a member he stood on an equal footing with all other members and stockholders.[1] Practically, however, as we shall see, he was, at least during the first twelve years of the Company's government, little better than a servant manipulated in the interest of the Company, held in servitude beyond a stipulated term, and defrauded of his just share in the proceeds of the undertaking.

The administration of Sir Thomas Smith, the first Treasurer of the Company, even when we allow for the exaggerated statements of the planters, was undoubtedly hurtful to the welfare of the infant colony. His policy was one of immediate gain. The success of the East India Company, whose first Governor he also was, as a trading corporation, probably led to his desire to conduct the Virginia Company on much the same principles. The welfare of the colonists was neglected, and the project of true colonization seems to have been lost sight of in the desire to exploit the riches of an unknown country and to discover the long sought-for passage to the South Seas. Though some £80,000 had been spent in twelve years, the Company, when turned over to Sir Edwin Sandys in 1619, was in debt £8000 or £9000, and there had survived but a bare fourth of near two thousand colonists that had been sent over.[2] Restrictions had been put upon the planting of corn, and the colonists were wholly dependent on the poor supplies from England or the doubtful generosity of the Indians. This policy had reduced the

---

[1] Va. Co. Rec., II., 94, 111. Stith, Append. 26. Later, when separate courts were established, subsequent to the charters of 1609 and 1612, for governing the Company, whenever members had a voice in these courts, the Virginia colonist enjoyed a like privilege, if he happened to be in England.

[2] Va. Co. Rec., I., 4, 64, 181. Va. Hist. Mag., Oct., 1893, 157. Of more than 800 colonists sent during the first three years, only about sixty survived; of a still larger number sent before 1619, but 400 were alive when Yeardley came, and half of these were unfit for work. Arber's Smith, Introd., cxxix.; Col. Rec. Va., 72, 80.

colony in 1609 to but fifty persons, and discontent with the aristocratical form of the Company's government and its bad administration led to a petition for a new charter. This charter constituted the London Company of Virginia a separate corporation from the Plymouth, defined the boundaries of its territory, and vested it with powers that gave it a more independent and republican character.[1]

To obtain fresh settlers the Company now issued broadsides and pamphlets, with specious promises, which, however honest its purpose, were certainly never fulfilled. There is evidence, however, in these advertisements to indicate that the Company consciously imposed on prospective settlers. One broadside solicits " workmen of whatever craft they may be—men as well as women, who have any occupation, who wish to go in this voyage for colonizing the country with people—they will receive for this voyage five hundred reales[2] for each one—houses to live in, vegetable gardens and orchards and also food and clothing at the expense of the Company—and besides this they will have a share of all the products and profits that may result from their labour, each in proportion, and they will also secure a share in the division of the land for themselves and their heirs forevermore."[3] A letter to the Lord Mayor, Aldermen and Companies of London offers similar terms and a definite grant of " one hundred acres for every man's person that hath a trade or a body able to endure days labour, as much for his child that are of yeares to do service to the colony with further particular reward according to their particular merits and industry." The full policy of the Company appears in a pamphlet issued by it about the same time; the object was to raise both men and money. Shares were set at twelve pounds ten shillings, and every " ordinary " man, woman and child above ten years that went to the colony to remain

---

[1] Stith, Append. 8; Nova Britannia, Force, I., 23.

[2] The equivalent of £12 10s., or the expense of transportation. Brown, I., 252.

[3] *Ibid.*, 248.

was allowed for his person a single share as if he had subscribed the required sum of money. Every "extraordinaire"
man, as Divines, Governors, Ministers of State and Justice,
"Knights, Gentlemen, Physitians," or such as were "of
worth for special services," were rated and registered by the
Council according to the value of their persons. The Company on its part agreed to bear all the charges of settling
and maintaining the plantation and furnishing supplies in a
joint stock for seven years. There was to be no private
trading, and "as we supply," they say, "from hence to the
Planters at our owne charge all necessaries for food and
apparel, for fortifying and building of houses in a joynt
stock so they are also to return from thence the encrease
and fruits of their labours for the use and advancement of
the same joynt stock till the end of seven years; at which
time we purpose (God willing) to make a division by Commissioners appointed of all the lands granted unto us by his
Majestie to every one of the colonists according to each
man's several adventure agreeing with our Register booke
which we doubt not will be for every share of twelve pounds,
ten shillings, five hundred acres at least." A large increase
of the stock is anticipated from the success of the colony,
"which stock is also (as the land) to be divided equally at
the seven years end or sooner, or so often as the Company
shall think fit for the greatness of it to make a dividend."
It was hoped that this would free them from further disbursements and would be an encouragement to the planters,
as their share in the profits would thus be larger from a
smaller number of shares owned by adventurers coming
into the dividend. In order to secure promptness in the
payment of subscriptions, every man was to be registered
according to the time his money or person began to adventure. The division of lands was to be just, and to insure this
it was to lie in scattered lots both good and bad, while the
commissioners were to be chosen equally by adventurers
and planters.

Regardless of these professions, when the seven years had

passed the Company proposed to allow only fifty acres of land to a share in a division of land about to be made, and alleged in excuse that they were not in possession of more, and that it was " not as yet freed from the encumber of woods and trees nor thoroughly survayed," yet they hoped " future opportunity will afford to divide the rest which we doubt not will bring at least *two* hundred acres to every single share." The division was in fact to be made not in performance of their obligations, but as a measure to raise further money for the expenses of the Company. No adventurer was to be permitted to share in the division unless he made a further subscription of £12 10s. (or more if he chose) to the Company's treasury. If he failed to do this he was to wait for some future division for his share, which would lie in some remote place and not along James river and " about the New Townes erected," as the lands of the present division did. The Company even went to the extent of admitting *new* adventurers, on a payment of the subscription, to equal shares in the division, in utter disregard of the rights of the old adventurers and of the planters in Virginia. Captain Argall was sent with commissioners and surveyors in 1616 to effect this division, and was granted in his own right a large plantation in the colony. It does not appear that the Virginia planters, except large shareholders like Captain John Martin and Lord Delaware, and possibly the men who had obtained their freedom in 1617 for building Charles City, ever participated in the division at all.[1]

No general private ownership of land in severalty seems to have existed in Virginia until the arrival of Yeardley as Governor in 1619. The body of the colonists were forcibly kept[2] out of their rights, and if they had estates, had no assur-

---

[1] Nova Brit., Force, I., 24, 25. New Brit., Brown, I., 273, 274. The charter of 1609 empowered the appointment of such a commission.

[2] Brown, II., 777, 778, 779. "A Brief Declaration," 1616; Va. Hist. Mag., Oct., 1893, 158. Discourse of the Old Company, 1625; Va. Co. Rec., II., 196; Winder MS., I., 16. In justice to the Company, however, it should be said that its finances were

ance of their titles before that time. Certain corporate rights
to land, however, belonged, as early as 1617, to such cor-

---

in a very bad state. They had suffered greatly from traducers
of the plantation both in England and Virginia. Many of the
original subscribers became so disheartened by this or the mis-
management of the Company that they refused to pay up their
subscriptions, and the Company was compelled to go into debt,
relying upon the private purses of its warmest supporters. The
state of affairs became so bad by 1612 that the Company took
care to secure in its third charter the insertion of a special
clause empowering them to collect subscriptions from its members. (Brown, II., 625.) In Nov. and Dec., 1610, on the report of Sir Thomas Gates of the imperative necessity of supplies, the Company determined that all adventurers, both those
already free of the Company (*i. e.*, who had paid up), and those
who desired to be free, should subscribe at least the sum of
£75, to be paid in three years, twenty-five each year, " towards
a newe supply to be sent for the relief of the said colony in
Virginia." Many members and other persons came to the relief of the Company, but a number of knights and gentlemen
who subscribed refused to pay, and the Company was forced
in 1613 to petition for the King's writ to sue in the High Court
of Chancery for the amounts due. Brown, II., 623-630, Brooke
to Elsmere.

Lotteries were also used as a means of obtaining ready money,
and in one to be drawn in 1614, every man who adventured £12
10s. in the lottery could have either his prize or a Bill of Adventure to Virginia, with his part in all lands and profits arising
from it. Adventurers who had not paid up their subscriptions
were permitted, on the payment to the Treasurer, in *money*, of
double the sum for which they had subscribed, both to be free
of the Company and to share in the lottery for the whole amount
paid in. If not satisfied with their drawings they could have
Bills of Adventure instead. The Company even declares that
if the colonists in Virginia were " now but a little while supplied with more hands and materials, we should the sooner
resolve upon a division of the country by lot, and so lessen the
General charge by leaving each several tribe or family to husband and manure his owne " (*Ibid.*, II., 762, 763, 764).

Whatever difficulties incident to a new plantation the Company may have had to overcome, these were undoubtedly enhanced by the maladministration of Sir Thomas Smith and his
officers. The accounts were left in such a disorderly state when
the government was turned over to Sandys that Smith's in-
tegrity was open to grave doubts. Though his accounts were
carefully examined and he was given an opportunity to clear
up the discrepancy, it was never satisfactorily explained. Va.
Co. Rec., I., 181; II., 83, 84, 251.

porations as Bermudas Hundreds, and a few "particular plantations" had been established by the common action of a number of adventurers or planters banded together in societies, sometimes with exceptional grants of jurisdiction that made them practically independent manors. Though the grants themselves in some cases dated as early as 1616, the establishment of these independent proprietaries was comparatively slow, and they increased in number very little before 1619.[1] The year 1616 seems to have marked a change in the policy of the Company toward land grants, and in general to the disadvantage of the colonist. When an actual division of land was made to shareholders in 1619 only those who had subscribed or had come to the colony before the departure of Dale in 1616 were considered to hold "Great Shares," or "Shares of Old Adventure," which entitled them to a grant of 100 acres, while the holders of shares issued since that time could claim but 50 acres a share.[2] Though a few exceptional grants were possibly

---

[1] Va. Mag. Hist. and Biog., Oct., 1893, 158, 160, Discourse of the Old Company. *Ibid.*, Oct., '94, 160, Instructions to Yeardley. MS. Rec. of Va. Co., III., 140; Robinson MS., 146; Winder MS., I., 16; Company's Register, 1615-23; Col. Rec. of Va., 20 *et seq.*, Va. Co. Rec., I., 62, 65.

The first of the societies known as Hundreds of any importance was Smith's Hundred, so called from Sir Thomas Smith, one of the subscribers to its fund, and it seems to have been established subsequently to April, 1618. In 1620 it became Southampton Hundred. Another was Martin's Hundred. Other plantations were established either by some ancient adventurer or planter, associating others with him, as Argall's, Martin's and Lord Delaware's plantations, or by new adventurers joining themselves under some one person, an example of which is seen in Christopher Lawne's plantation. The failure of the Company itself as a successful colonizing agent and its very weak financial condition was the sole occasion of this private enterprise.

[2] No dividend, except of lands, was ever declared in favor of the colonists, nor is there any record of a division of profits amongst the adventurers generally. The division of land that was made fell far short of the promises of the Company under which the shares were taken. The Ancient Planters, by the Company's orders, in 1619 were to have the 100 acres as a first

made to individuals by governors before Yeardley, they had
no assurance of their titles, and we can regard no earlier
date than 1619 as that of the full and general establishment
of the rights of private property in land in Virginia.[1]

This communal system continued without a break until
the year 1613, when a variation was introduced in the conditions of service of a number of the colonists and in their
relation to the land. A sort of qualified property right was
given them by the introduction of a tenancy-at-will on small

division, and a future increase of this was promised only to
those who had gone at their own charge. Their rights to be
favored above those who went after the greatest hardships
were over were apparently recognized by the Instructions, but
they themselves in their first Assembly seem to have felt sufficient doubt as to its possible construction to petition the Company that "they have the second, third and more divisions as
well as any other planter," and shares also for their male children and *issue.* The latter request was not granted, but they
appear to have been put on equal footing with other planters
in subsequent land grants, which depended on a peopling of
the tract first granted. I can find no evidence of a second or
third division ever having been made. Arber's Smith, 526; Va.
Hist. Mag., Oct., '94, 156, 157; Va. Co. Rec., I., 14, 15; Stith,
139; Col. Rec. Va., Assembly of 1619.

[1] I can find no authority whatever, except an erroneous read-
ing of Stith (p. 139), for Chalmers' assertion that private property in land was instituted by Dale in Virginia in the year
1615 by a grant of 50 acres in fee to every free man in the
colony. All the evidence we have proves conclusively that no
such grant of lands was made, nor does Stith ascribe the change
in the Company's policy at this time to Dale; it was the result,
however, of the prosperous condition of the colony, which was
largely the work of Dale. Dale was in England June 12, 1616,
probably before the time of the issue of the Brief Declaration
relating to the dividend of 50 acres, and it is possible if this
were so that he was consulted in the matter. There is no authority, however, for the statement that it was due to his
influence. From the "Declaration" itself it seems to have been
dictated by other motives. Chalmers gives Stith as his authority on this point, and the mistake has crept into Virginia his-
tories on the sole authority of Chalmers. He further errs in
the date, while Stith gives it correctly. Stith, 139; Chalmers'
Pol. Annals, 36; Campbell, 116; Cooke, 110; Burke, I., 177; Doyle,
Va., Md. and the Carolinas, 152.

I

tracts of land belonging to the Company, either at a fixed rent or on certain conditions of service to the colony.[1]

This change was brought about by the intolerable conditions of servitude and the right which the few remaining colonists of 1607 probably had to demand a release under their five-year contracts now expired. The Bermuda planters petitioned Governor Gates for permission to plant corn for a subsistence, as the Company had been derelict in furnishing supplies. This petition was denied unless they accepted a tenantship-at-will, paying a yearly rent of three barrels of corn and giving a month's service to the colony.[2] The condition of the rest of the colonists was less fortunate; they were either *retained* in their servitude or granted, as tenants, small farms on condition of giving eleven months of the year to the benefit of the common store, from which they received but two barrels of corn.

By 1616 further modifications had taken place, chiefly in favor of the farmer class, who had become a source of profit to the Company and now numbered nearly a third of the colonists. The time of their service was reduced to thirty-one days, rendered at their convenience, and they were allowed to rent laborers from the colony as their servants. They paid a small rent for their farms and were responsible for their own maintenance and that of their servants. These laborers were men transported at the Company's charge, and could be disposed of by the Governor for the best interests of the colony, as their maintenance would otherwise devolve upon the Company. Governor Dale placed a number of these on a tract of land called the " common garden," and applied the proceeds of their labor to the maintenance of their overseers and the public officers of the colony. The skilled laborers and artificers, such as carpenters and smiths, constituted another class and worked at their trades for the

---

[1] Stith, 131, 132; Chalmers, 34; Purchas, 1766 (Hamor).

[2] Decl. of Anc. Planters, Col. Rec. of Va., 75; Chalmers, 39; Stith, 132; Purchas, 1766.

colony, while they had land and time allotted them to till ground for their maintenance.[1] The freedom thus given to officers, farmers and skilled laborers was only conditional, depending on a responsibility for their own maintenance, while full control continued to be exercised over those who depended on the Company for support. This system continued without any important change until 1619.

Some distinction of classes existed in the colony from the earliest days. Society was influenced by its personnel, and doubtless also by the fact that many of the colonists, unable to pay their transportation, were either sent upon the common charge of the Company or of adventurers in England. Many of the gentlemen among the first immigrants took with them valets and servants on stipulated wages. The Company also, beside its seamen and soldiers, had servants in its employ on wages.[2] This class, however, was small and exceptional, and the bulk of the colonists went as members of the Company, either at their own charge or at the charge of the Company or of some private person. The hardships of the early years left little opportunity for the growth of an aristocratic sentiment, though we find the distinctions of class frequently recognized and the offices absorbed by a limited number of gentlemen. Beyond this, little practical distinction existed. All were colony servants alike and suffered much the same exactions.

Up to 1613 they were worked as hirelings of the Company, receiving but a miserable support in lieu of their services. A portion of them, we have seen, then became tenants on the Company's land on hard conditions of tenure.

---

[1] Va. Hist. Reg., I., 107-110, Rolf's Relation, 1616; Purchas, Pilgrimes, 1766, Hamor's Narrative; Purchas, His Pilgrimage, 837; Va. Co. Rec., I., 65. The farms consisted of three acres, and the rental of a servant was two barrels and a half of corn.

[2] Smith, Hist. of Va., I., 241; Neil, London Co., 13, Early Settlement; Third Rept. of Royal Comm. on Hist. MSS., Appd., 53; Arber's Smith, 107, 122, 448, 486, 487, cxxix.; MS. Rec. Va. Co., III., 142; Brown, II., 550.

Others, through the influence of Dale, were induced to serve the colony in the " building of Charles City and Hundred "[1] three years longer, on the promise of absolute freedom from the " general and common servitude" so much abhorred. They were allowed but a month in the year and a day in the week to provide for themselves, and were afterwards deprived of half of this time, so that they were forced, as they say, " out of our daily tasks to redeem time wherein to labour for our sustenance thereby miserably to purchase our freedom."[2] The favored Bermuda planters were finally given a charter of incorporation and enjoyed better terms, but were bound to the performance of certain duties for a limited time before they could have their freedom.[3]

When Lord Delaware came in 1610 with fresh supplies he thoroughly organized the colony as a labor force under commanders and overseers.[4] Dale afterwards applied a rigorous military system adopted from the Low Countries, and enforced it with great severity in carrying out his plans for establishing new plantations. The colonists were marched to their daily work in squads and companies under officers, and the severest penalties were prescribed for a breach of discipline or neglect of duty. A persistent neglect of labor was to be punished by galley service from one to three years. Penal servitude was also instituted; for " petty offences " they worked " as slaves in irons for a term of years." The planters affirm that there were " continual whippings and extraordinary punishments," such as hanging, shooting, breaking on the wheel, and even burning alive, but it is likely they much exaggerated the state of affairs. The system at least proved salutary. Towns were built and palis-

---

[1] Col. Rec. Va., 68, 81.

[2] Stith, 132; Purchas, Pilgrimes, 1766; Col. Rec. Va., 75, 76. " Having most of them served the colony six or seven years in that general slavery."

[3] Va. Hist. Reg., I., 100, Rolf's Relation, 1616.

[4] Lord Delaware's Letter to the Patentees in England, July 7, 1610; Hist. of Travaile into Virginia Britannia, Introd., Hakluyt Soc., 34.

aded, and the colony was reduced to thorough order.[1] Under the arbitrary rule of Governor Argall this system was to some extent revived. " Three years' slavery " to the colony was the penalty for a violation of his edicts, and absence from church was punished with " slavery " from a week to a year and a day.[2]

No freedom was granted from the common servitude until March, 1617, when the three-year contract made by Dale with the men of Charles City Hundred had expired and they demanded their " long desired freedome from that general and common servitude." Governor Yeardley willingly assented to this reasonable request, as they had now served the colony for nine or ten years.[3] No further extensive grant of freedom was made until he came as Governor in 1619, bringing a proclamation of freedom to most of the ancient planters. Whenever it was obtained before this it was only at an " extraordinary payment," and throughout the first administration of Yeardley and that of Argall the great majority of the colonists remained in their former condition, which the ancient planters with little exaggeration termed " noe waye better than slavery."[4] Their rights as English-

---

[1] Col. Rec. Va., 68, 69, 81; Force, III., 1647, Laws; Cal. State Papers, Col. 39. Dale's justification is to be found in the character of the colonists with whom he had to deal. Cf. Letter Dale to Salisbury, Brown, I., 506.

[2] See MS. Rec. Va. Co., III., 143, for a number of these edicts. Two instances may serve to illustrate the policy of her government. Goods were to be sold to the colonists from the magazine at 25 per cent. profit, while the price of tobacco was fixed at 3 shillings. A violation of this edict was punished with three years' servitude to the colony. " Every person to go to church Sundays and holydays or lye neck and heel on the corps du guard the night following and be a slave the week following, second offence a month, third offence a year and a day."

[3] Col. Rec. Va., 77; MS. Rec. Va. Co., III., 142.

[4] Col. Rec. Va., 75, 78, 81. " Good Newes from Virginia," 11, 21, 32 and E. D. The numerous letters sent by the Governor and General Assembly, 1621-1623, to prevent a re-establishment of Sir Thomas Smith's government in the Company, while expressed in extravagant language, bear witness to the very ar-

men, guaranteed by the first charter of the Company, had practically no recognition before the arrival of Yeardley.

In 1618 the popular party in the Virginia Company triumphed over the court party, and Sir Thomas Smith was ousted from the governorship and Sir Edwin Sandys elected in his stead. An almost complete change of policy was the result; a new Governor was sent in the person of Yeardley to supplant the rapacious Argall. Yeardley carried with his commission an important concession of rights to the Virginia planters. A new regime of freedom and representative government, coupled with full rights of private property in land and a responsible governorship, now began in the colony Yeardley did not bring freedom to all the ancient planters, but only to all those who had gone at their own charge previous to the departure of Dale in 1616, and to those who, sent at the Company's charge, had already served the full time of their servitude to the colony.[1] Many were, however, still retained in servitude until the end of their terms, and the Company, until its dissolution in 1624, continued to send others at the Company's charge on terms of servitude modified to suit the changed conditions in the colony.

We see, then, that the colonist, while in theory only a Vir-

---

bitrary treatment of the colonists during the first twelve years of the Company. Facts were attested by many persons who had been actual sufferers, and affirm that many of those whose lives had been recklessly sacrificed were not of mean rank, as alleged by Smith and Alderman Johnson, but of "ancient houses and born to estates of £1,000 by the year, some more, some less who likewise perished by famine, those who survived who had both adventured their estates and persons were constrained to serve the colony (as if they had been slaves) seven or eight years for their freedoms who underwent as hard service and labors as the basest fellow that was brought out of Newgate." " Rather than be reduced to live under like government," they say, " we desire his Majestie that Commissioners may be sent over with authority to hang us." Winder MSS., I., 47-52. Cf. *Ibid.*, 30, and MS. Rec. Va. Co., III., 168, 179, 180, 235. Cf. " Good Newes from Virginia," II., 21, 32 sq.

[1] Va. Hist. Mag., Oct., 1894, 157.

ginia member of the London Company, and entitled to equal
rights and privileges with other members or adventurers,
was, from the nature of the case, practically debarred from
exercising these rights. As a planter absent in Virginia he
could not sit nor have a voice in the councils of the Company; he was entirely dependent on the Company's good
faith for the performance of its obligations, and had recourse
to no means to enforce their performance. He was kept by
force in the colony,[1] and could have no communication with
his friends in England. His letters were intercepted by the
Company and could be destroyed if they contained anything
to the Company's discredit. He was completely at the
mercy of the edicts of arbitrary governors, and was forced
to accept whatever abridgment of his rights and contract
seemed good to the Governor and the Company.[2] His true
position was that of a common servant working in the interest of a commercial company. In lieu of his support, or of
his transportation and support, he was bound to the service
of this company for a term of years. Under the arbitrary
administration of the Company and of its deputy governors
he was as absolutely at its disposal as a servant at his master's. His conduct was regulated by corporal punishment
or more extreme measures. He could be hired out by the
Company to private persons, or by the Governor for his
personal advantage.

Suggested by the policy of the Company, there gradually
grew up after the year 1616 and the establishment of separate
plantations, the practice on the part of societies of planters,
and later of private persons, of transporting servants to settle and work their lands very much on the same conditions

---

[1] Not till winter of 1616-17 was any freedom to return to England given to the Virginia colonists. Brown, II., 798.

[2] The charter of 1609, which gave the Company a more independent government, was of no advantage to the colonists, as
the Governors appointed were given arbitrary powers. Col. Rec.
of Va., 75, 76; Stith, 132, 147, 148; Arber's Smith, cxxix.,
488; Force, III., 16.

of service as those made by the Company.[1] This developed, as property began to be acquired by the planters generally, into the common mode of transporting servants on contracts by indenture for a limited time of service, varying in individual cases according to the terms of the contract.[2]

In 1619, under the new Governor of the Company, an important modification was introduced regarding its servants in Virginia and colonists who should be afterwards transported at the common charge. The plan instituted by Dale of making a part of the colonists farmers or tenants at a fixed rent, and others servants on a large tract of land for the Company's use, had worked successfully in raising revenues for the government, and the Company now proposed, by an extension of this experiment, to relieve the colonists "forever of all taxes and public burthens," by setting apart large tracts of "publick land" to be worked by a system of tenantship-at-halves. Such a system had been commended to Governor Argall in 1617, and orders had been issued setting apart various tracts of land, but the provisions were not carried out until the governorship of Yeardley, when tracts of three thousand acres were set apart in each of the four boroughs, and a special tract of like size was reserved for the Governor at Jamestown. These were for the general

---

[1] Va. Co. Rec., II., 32, 41, 42, 196.

[2] It is impossible to say just when the first actually "indented" servants were introduced into Virginia. They became a distinct class after 1619, and formal indentures were probably in use that year applying to servants sent to the planters. The Assembly of 1619 provided that all contracts of servants should be recorded and enforced. Whether indentures had been used by the Company or private persons previous to this is not clear. They seem to have been applied to the Company's tenants after 1619. The manuscript records of the Company contain a reference, under the date 1622, to a boy's indenture, and it is probable indentures were used in 1619. A registry was kept of persons transported in the Company's ships, but those sent otherwise by private persons were not included in it until 1622, when so much trouble had been occasioned by verbal contracts that the Company's bookkeeper was required henceforth to register all contracts for service. Col. Rec., 21, 28; Va. Co. Rec., II., 17, 23.

revenue of the government. Other tracts of half the size, called " borough lands," were given as common lands to each borough for the support of their " particular magistrates and officers and of all other charges." For endowing a " university and college " ten thousand acres were allotted in the territory of Henrico.[1] Men were to be placed on the land as tenants-at-halves on contract to remain there seven years, returning half the profits of their labor to the Company and enjoying the other half themselves. They were apportioned as the revenues to be raised demanded, and increased from time to time. Within less than a year 500 persons were sent on these terms.[2] Not only were the old public offices, such as the governor's and secretary's, to be thus supported by the allotment of a fixed number of tenants, which must be kept intact by successive incumbents, but whenever a new office was created or any project of public importance undertaken this became the common mode of insuring its support.[3]

By a special application of the English system of apprenticeship, well established in England after the Statute of Apprentices of Elizabeth, 1563, which put a premium upon agricultural apprenticeship, an attempt was made to round out this tenantship and insure its perpetuity. One hundred poor boys and girls who were about to starve in the streets of London were sent in 1619, by the aid of the mayor and council of the city, to be bound to the tenants for a term of years, at the end of which they were to become themselves

---

[1] Instructions to Governor Yeardley, 1618; Va. Hist. Mag., Oct., 1894, 155, 156, 158, 159; MS., Libr. of Supreme Court, Wash. Va. Rec., cap. 23, 221, p. 72.

[2] Va. Co. Rec., I., 22, 26; Stith, 163, 165; Force, III., No. 5, 10; *Ibid.*, 82; Collingwood MS., I., 30-35.

[3] Va. Co. Rec., 45, 59, 111, 119, 130-137, 151, 152. *Ibid.*, MS. Rec., III., 123, 161, 170. The office of the marshal, vice-admiral and treasurer, when created, were to be so supported; the " physician general " had tenants, and the ministers also six apiece for their glebes. The support of the East India school, of the iron works and of a glass furnace was to be provided for on the same plan.

tenants-at-halves on the public lands, with an allowance of stock and corn to begin with. Industrial apprenticeship was also provided for to encourage trade and to stop the excessive planting of tobacco. The term was usually limited to seven years, or in the case of girls, upon marriage or becoming of age. Apprentices soon began to be disposed of to the planters on their reimbursing the Company for the charges of their outfit and transportation, and the records in several cases suggest a suspicion of speculation.[1]

The intent was probably to establish a kind of *metayer* system, though the tenant was at liberty at the expiration of his term to remove to " any other place at his owne will and pleasure." It was supposed that the terms were sufficiently advantageous to induce him to enter into further contracts for successive periods of seven years. The success of the earlier plan introduced by Dale led the Company to hope not only for the support of the government, but for large returns in excess, and the design was to make it a permanent and certain source of all the necessary revenues. It was frustrated, however, by the maladministration of the system on the part of the government and officers. The tenants were frequently seated on remote and barren lands, or defrauded in their contracts, being taken from their places and hired by the year to planters, so that almost from the beginning the system was a failure, and instead of providing a revenue it was not even self-supporting. The public tenants were particularly neglected in favor of those belonging to the officers, and several propositions were made at differ-

[1] Cal. S. P., Col. 19; Neill, London Co., 160, note, 161, 235; Cunningham, II., 42; Robinson MS., 68; MS. Rec. Va. Co., III., 162; Va. Co. Rec., I., 25, 36, 39, 40-42, 91, 97, 100, 124, 140, 169.

[2] Force, III., No. 5, 14, 15; Va. Co. Rec., I., 40-42; Hening, I., 230. Though the Company was forced by the city of London to grant exceptional terms to tenants who had been formerly apprentices, by assigning them at the expiration of their tenantship a land grant of twenty-five acres in fee, yet it stipulated for the privilege of re-engaging them for further terms if the tenant freely consented.

ent times for a change in the terms of tenantship, but it was never effected. The system practically came to an end with the dissolution of the Company in 1624, but even as late as 1642 some few tenants remained, showing that the Company's plan of renewal of terms had been practiced.[1] It had degenerated by this time into the payment of a fixed rent or into planting for the benefit of the owner.[2] The growth of a class of strictly indented servants was also a factor in the failure of this tenantship. Servants were much less costly, and rapidly became more profitable.[3] Fifty servants were sent to serve the public in 1619, and in the next year a hundred more, say the records, "to be disposed of among the old planters which they exceedingly desire and will pay the Company their charges with very great thanks."[4] These men had been selected with great care, but the Company was unfortunate in being forced by the repeated orders of King James to add a number of dissolute persons whom he was determined, by the exercise of mere prerogative, to remove from England as an undesirable class.[5]

---

[1] Va. Co. Rec., I., 117, 169, 173; Smith, II., 40, 106, 107; Va. Co. Rec. MS., III., 161, 163, 166, 170, July 5, 1621; Va. Hist. Reg., I., 159; Hen.. I., 230; Appd. 8th Rept. Royal Com. on Hist. MSS., pts. II. & III., 39-44. Geo. Sandys, March 30, 1623, writes to his brother, Sir Samuel Sandys: "The tenants sent on that so absurd condition of halves were neither able to sustain themselves nor to discharge their moiety, and so dejected with their scarce provisions and finding nothing to answer their expectations, that most of them gave themselves over and died of melancholy, the rest running so far in debt as left them still behind-hand and many (not seldom) losing their crops while they hunted for their belly." Cf. Nichols to Worsenholme, p. 41.

[2] Robinson MS., 188.

[3] Va. Co. Rec., I., 87; MS., *Ibid.*, III., 171; Neill, London Co., 230; Force, III., 14. The average cost of a tenant was 16, of a servant 6 pounds.

[4] Va. Co. Rec., I., 67, 83.

[5] Stith, 165, 167, 168; Neill, London Co., 163; Va. Co. Rec., I., 25, 26, 33, 34. The Company was ordered to send the " men prest " in Nov., 1619, but it postponed doing so for nearly two months, in the hope of being relieved of the necessity. The

The new life which began in Virginia in the year 1619 greatly encouraged industry and husbandry and led to a large increase of independent proprietaries in a few years. Special inducements were offered by large grants of land and exceptional privileges to associations of planters and adventurers for the establishing of separate plantations. Liberal grants were also made to tradesmen and to members of the Company in proportion to their shares. To encourage immigration additional grants were made to them for every person transported to the colony in the next seven years, A large number of servants and tenants was needed on these plantations, and for some time the importation by private persons was larger than that by the Company.[2] In 1619 the number of tenants and servants was sufficiently large to make necessary some regulation of the future conditions of their servitude by law. The first General Assembly of Virginia held in that year gave legal sanction and recognition to the servitude by the passage of special enactments providing for the recording and strict performance of all contracts between master and servant. The right of free marriage was limited in the case of female servants, and servants in general were prohibited from trade with the Indians. Corporal punishment was provided as a penalty in cases where a free man suffered fine unless the master remitted the fine, and a general discretionary power was given to the Governor and Council for regulation of other cases.[3]

importunity of the king, however, compelled it to yield. One hundred persons had been included in the first order, but it is probable that only half of these were sent to Virginia, and they were allowed to be selected. The Somers Island Company probably yielded to the request of the Virginia Company and took the rest. Collingwood MS., I., 47.

[1] Va. Hist. Mag., 160, 162, 164 (Oct., 1894); Col. Rec. Va., 78, 81; Va. Co. Rec., I., 39; II., 124, 128, 196.

[2] *Ibid.*, I., 123, 137, 148, 153, 154, 161; II., 148, 150. In the four years 1619-23 forty-four patents were issued to as many different people for the transportation of a hundred persons each to Virginia; in the twelve years preceding only six patents had been granted.

[3] Col. Rec. Va., 1, 21, 24, 25, 28; Laws, 1619.

The main principles on which the institution of servitude was based were by this time clearly developed, and its growth henceforth consisted in the gradual addition of incidents originating in customs peculiar to colonial conditions, which, recognized by judicial decisions, became fixed in local customary law, or by the enactment of special statutes were established as a part of the statutory law.

I

CHAPTER II.

In the policy of the London Company towards its colonists during the first twelve years we have seen the beginning and gradual development of an idea which, adopted and amplified by the later government of the Company and in the administration of Virginia as a Royal Colony, grew into the system here called Indented Servitude, which throughout the colonial period was widely extended in all the American colonies and became an important factor in their economic and social development. Gradually, and not always consciously, it was formed into a hard and fixed system, in some respects analogous to the later institution of slavery, from which, however, it was always broadly distinguished both in social custom and in law.

The servitude thus developed was limited and conditional. With respect to its origin it was of two kinds, resting on distinct principles:

First. Voluntary Servitude, based on free contract with the London Company or with private persons for definite terms of service, in consideration of the servant's transportation and maintenance during servitude.

Second. Involuntary Servitude, where legal authority condemned a person to a term of servitude judged necessary for his reformation or prevention from an idle course of life, or as a reprieve from other punishment for misdemeanors already committed.

Though involuntary on the part of the servant, this kind

---

[1] The term Indented Servitude has been used as the one best characteristic of the system at large. Strictly indented servants not only formed the largest class, but gave legal definiteness to the system of white servitude.

involved a contract between the authority imposing the sentence and the person that undertook the transportation of the offender,[1] and the master's right to service resting upon the terms of this contract made or assigned to him was practically on the same footing as involuntary servitude.

The great body of servants was comprised in the former class. They were free persons, largely from England, Wales, Scotland and Ireland, who wished to go to the colony as settlers to better their condition, but were too poor to bear the charges of their transportation.[2] They consequently entered into a voluntary contract with any one that would assume these charges and their maintenance for such a term of years as would repay the outlay, placing themselves for this limited time at the disposal of the person for any reasonable service. The contract was made in Great Britain with resident planters or the agents of colonists, but more frequently with shipmasters who traded in Virginia and disposed of the servant on their arrival as they saw fit. The agreement was by deed indented, and hence arose the term "Indented" Servants.[3] This class of so-called "Kids" was

---

[1] The right to the stipulated term of servitude was given to *any one* that would contract for the servant's transportation, and he seems to have had free disposal of this right when he reached Virginia. Va. Co. Rec., I., 91; II., 10, 11; Eng. Statutes at Large, 4 Geo., c. II.; Anson, 7, 43. This was probably in England a Contract of Record.

[2] Jefferson's Works, IX., 254 sq.; Jones, Present State, 53, 54.

[3] Neill, Va. Carolorum, 57, note. An indenture of 1628, made after assignments of contracts were recognized in Virginia, may be taken as typical of those generally in use. A husbandman of Surrey County, England, contracts and binds himself to a citizen and ironmonger of London " to continue the Obedient Servant of him, the said Edward hurd his heirs and assignes and so by him or them sente transported unto the countrey and land of Virginia in the parts beyond the seas to be by him or them employde upon his plantation there for and during the space of ffour yeares—and will be tractable and obedient and a good and faithful servant onyst to be in all such things as shall be Commanded him—In consideration whereof the said Edward hurd doth covenant that he will transporte and furnishe to the said Logwood to and for Virginia aforesaid—and allowe unto him sustenance meat and drink apparel and other necessaryes for his livelyhood and sustenance during the said service "—sealed and delivered in the presence of two servants.

supplemented by a smaller class of persons who went on agreements for fixed wages for a definite time.

The other large class was supplied chiefly from English paupers, vagrants and dissolute persons sent under the arbitrary exercise of royal prerogative or by court sentences, and later by the action of English penal statutes. In the earlier years it included a large number of poor children from the counties and towns of England, who were sent to apprenticeship on easy conditions.[1] The penal regulations of the colony up to the year 1642 tended also to recruit this class.[2] A very large number of the convicts sent to the American plantations were political and not social criminals. Of the Scotch prisoners taken at the battle of Worcester sixteen hundred and ten were sent to Virginia in 1651. Two years later a hundred Irish Tories were sent, and in 1685 a number of the followers of Monmouth that had escaped the cruelties of Jeffreys. Many of the Scotch prisoners of Dunbar and of the rebels of 1666 were sent to New England[3] and the other plantations. As early as 1611 Governor Dale, anxious to fill out the number of two thousand men for establishing military posts along James river, had recommended that all convicts from the common jails be kept up for three years. They "are not always," he said, "the worst kind of men, either for birth, spirit, or body and would be glad to escape a just sentence and make this their new country, and plant therein with all diligence, cheerfulness and comfort." This request passed unheeded, and the earliest

---

[1] Cal. State Papers, Domestic, 584; Stith, 108. Blackstone, I., 137, note; IV., 401 and note; Reeves, 598.

[2] The servitude for offenses, early instituted by the governors and continued by the courts, can hardly be regarded as properly a part of the system, however. It was strict penal servitude in the interest of the commonweal. These convicts were not held by the colonists, but employed on public works as servants of the colony, or in service to the Governor in his official capacity, except in specific cases. Robinson MS., II., 12, 13, 65; Va. Co. MS. Rec., III., 215, 224. Cf. Hening, I., 351; II., 119, 441; III., 277.

[3] Mass. Hist. Coll., Vol. IX., 2, Dale to Salisbury.

introduction of any of the criminal class seems to have been in 1618, when a man convicted of manslaughter and sentenced to be hanged was reprieved, "because he was a carpenter and the plantation needed carpenters."[1] In the early years of the seventeenth century England suffered, particularly in her border counties, from a number of malefactors whom it was impossible to bring to justice. Magistrates and most of the gentlemen of the counties countenanced them, and even had them in their employ for private ends. Many schemes were proposed to the king for remedying the evil and compelling the justices and officers to perform their duty. Transportation had been made use of before, and the king now proposed to send the offenders to Virginia.[2] From 1618 to 1622 a number came, but the large increase was in the latter half of the century. In 1653 an order of the Council of State appointed a committee concerning the transportation of vagrants to the foreign plantations. In 1661 another committee was appointed to further the sending of people, and power was given to Justices of the Peace to transport felons, beggars and disorderly persons.[3]

Sufficient numbers had been sent under this power, and by the transportation of political offenders, to furnish ringleaders for an attempt to subvert the government in 1663. In consequence of this and the danger of the continued importation of "great numbers" of these "wicked villaines," the General Court, upon the petition of the counties of Gloucester and Middlesex, issued an order prohibiting any further importation of them after the twentieth of January, 1671.[4] Through the influence of Lord Arlington this order

---

[1] *Ibid.*, 1-4; Middlesex Rec., II., 224. Others were granted reprieves earlier on condition of transportation, but it is probable that they went elsewhere than Virginia. Sir Thomas Smith was Governor of the East India Company at this time.

[2] Surtees Soc., Vol. 68, 419, 420, Appd.; Bacon, Essay on Plantations.

[3] Cal. State Papers, Col. 28, 441; cf. Ashley, Economic Hist. Eng., 366.

[4] Rec. Genl. Ct., 1670-2, 5, 52; Hening, II., 191; Rob. MS., 8, 67, 257, 261.

was confirmed in England and was made to apply to the other American colonies as well as to Virginia.[1] A strict system of search was applied to every ship that entered Virginia ports, and for the next half-century the colony had a respite from this class of " Newgaters " and " Jail Birds."[2] Their transportation was now diverted to the West Indies, but this proved so ineffectual in putting a stop to petty felonies that in the 4th year of George I. (1717) Parliament passed a statute over the most vigorous protests from the Virginia merchants in London, making the American colonies practically a reformatory and a dumping-ground for the felons of England.[3] In 1766 the benefits of this act were extended to include Scotland, though Benjamin Franklin, on the part of Pennsylvania, memorialized Parliament against it, and in 1768 the more speedy transportation of felons was ordered.[4] The practice was only stopped by the War of the Revolution. The preamble of the act of 1779 significantly remarks that "whereas the transportation of felons to His Majesty's American Colonies is attended with many difficulties," they are now to be sent to "other parts beyond the sea, whether situate in America or not."[5] They were finally disposed of in convict galleys or sent to the new penal colonies in New South Wales or at Botany Bay.[6]

Virginia, contrary to some of the colonies, never favored the importation of this class. They were seldom reformed, and their " room ' was held much more desirable than their " company," says Jones.[7] Many attempts were made to pre-

---

[1] Cal. State Papers, 242; Rec. Genl. Ct., 52.

[2] Rec. Genl. Ct., Apl. 6, 1672, 52.

[3] Geo. I., c. 11, Statutes at Large; Va. MSS. fr. B. R. O., Vol. II., pt. 2, p. 579.

[4] 6 Geo. III., c. 32; Ford, Works of Franklin, Vol. X., 120; 8 Geo. III., c. 15.

[5] 8 Geo. III., c. 74.

[6] Lecky, England in the Eighteenth Century, VI., 254.

[7] Jones, Present State, 53, 54; Beverley, 233; " Va. Verges," 1622.

vent their coming by the imposition of heavy duties, but they were not finally and effectually prohibited until 1788.[1] The ability given the States to lay a tax of $10 on all persons imported was incorporated into the Constitution of the United States, mainly through the efforts of George Mason of Virginia, and was partly designed to keep out convicts.[2] From this attitude of the colony it probably received a much smaller number than some of the other colonies.[3]

Another important source of involuntary servitude was found in the practice of " spiriting," which grew up in the reign of Charles I. and continued throughout the Commonwealth period and the reign of Charles II. It was an organized system of kidnapping persons, young and old, usually of the laboring classes, and transporting them to the plantations to be sold for the benefit of the kidnapper or shipmaster to whom they were assigned.[4] It became widely extended in England, but Bristol and London were the centers of the traffic. Throughout London and the parishes of Middlesex county its agents, called " spirits," were distributed; men and women, yeomen, tradesmen, doctors and a class of rogues and idlers who earned a livelihood by this means.[5] The ladies of the court, and even the mayor of

---

[1] Va. MSS. fr. B. R. O., 1697, p. 320; 1723, 1729, March 26; Hening, XII., 668. Cf. III., 251; V., 24, 546.

[2] Madison Papers, Vol. III., 1430; Article I., sec. 9, Constitution of U. S.

[3] Lodge, Colonies, 242; Lecky, VI., 254 sq. Franklin's Works, X., 119.

[4] Middlesex Records, III., 38, 94, 245. The offense, when discovered, which was probably not true of one in twenty cases, was treated with remarkable leniency by the courts. Under the Civil Law it would have been punished with death, but we meet with petty fines of a few shillings, even when the " spirit " confessed the crime, and in one case only 12d.; a few hours in the pillory, or imprisonment till the fine was paid seems to have been considered by the judges a sufficient atonement. The Session Rolls of Middlesex show that a large number of the cases were not even brought to trial, though true bills had been brought against the offenders.

[5] Middlesex Rec., II., 306, 326, 335, 336; III., 100, 184, 229, 253, 257, 259, 271, 326, &c.; IV., 40, 70-87, 245; Cal. State Papers, Col. 411.

Bristol, were not beneath the suspicion of profiting by this lucrative business. All manner of pretenses were used to decoy the victims aboard ships lying in the Thames or to places where they could be assaulted and forcibly conveyed on board, to be disposed of to the ship's company or to merchants.[1]

The practice first arose in connection with the West India plantations. Barbadoes and other island plantations probably received a much greater number than the American colonies.[2] We find a case belonging to Virginia as early as 1644.[3] In 1664 the abuse had grown so bad that tumults were frequently raised in the streets of London. It was only necessary to point the finger at a woman and call her a "common spirit" to raise a "ryot" against her. The Lord Mayor and aldermen of London, and a number of merchants, planters and shipmasters, sent petitions urging the establishment of a registry office to put an end to the practice.[4] The office was established in September of that year, and was to register all covenants and issue certificates to the merchants.[5] The penalty for not registering any person who was to be transported as a servant was £20, and the consent of friends or relatives in person at the office was necessary for the transportation of any one under twelve years of age, and good reasons had to be shown for such transportation. Even these strict regulations failed to stop the practice, and in 1670 it was necessary to resort to Parliament to prevent the abuse by imposing as a penalty death without benefit of clergy.[6]

---

[1] *Ibid.*, 449; Va. MS. fr. B. R. O., 1640-91, 170.

[2] Middlesex Rec., Vol. III., 276; IV., 65, 69-73, 78, 79, 155, 196, 245.

[3] Va. MSS. fr. the British Record Office, Vol. I., 46. Cf. State Papers (Calendar), 411, 457.

[4] Cal. State Papers, Col. 220; Middlesex Rec., IV., 181.

[5] Cal. State Papers, Col. 221, 232. The office had been proposed in 1660.

[6] This and the lessened demand for servants was sufficient to put an end to the abuse.

Further technical distinctions arose in law determined by the title under which servitude was due. Thus, where verbal contracts alone existed, or where it was specially stipulated for, " Servitude according to the Custom " took place, and the servant was held for the customary term, whatever it might be, unless a contract was proved. After the statute of 1643, which set a definite term for all servants brought in without indentures, this became known as *servitude by act of Assembly.* Spirited servants, as a rule, came under this act. The servitude of felons and convicts, after the penal statutes, was known as servitude by act of Parliament, and that of offenders sentenced in Virginia as servitude by order of court. These distinctions were of little practical importance, however, as all servants except convicts met with the same treatment both in social custom and in law.

The servants in Virginia were usually English, Scotch or Irish, but there were also a few Dutch, French, Portuguese and Polish.[1] They were usually transported persons, but

---

[1] Jones, 54; Robinson MS., II., 255; Howe, Va., 207. Before the statute of 1661, which made negroes generally slaves, a number were held as servants for a term, and even afterward a few seem to have remained servants. Robinson MS., 10, 30, 250, 256; MS. Rec. Va. Co., III., 292; MS. Rec. Genl. Ct., 161, 218; 1673, 1675. From 1656-1676 and after 1691, Indian children sold by their parents, and captives, could legally be held only as servants; but the disposition was, when not restrained by law, to make them slaves. Acts of 1676 and 1682 legalized Indian slavery, but it was prohibited in 1670, and finally in 1691 by an act for free trade with all Indians, which the General Court construed as taking away all right to their slavery. Many were, however, unjustly reduced to slavery up to 1705, as the act was supposed to date from the revisal of 1705, and not from 1691. Hening, I., 396; II., 15, 143, 155, 283, 491, 562; III., 69 and note. Robinson MS., 256, 261, 262; MS. Rec. Genl. Ct., 29, 218. (*Vid.* Jeff. Cases in Genl. Court, p. 123; Robin *et al.* vs. Hardaway, 1772.) Mulatto bastards were also made servants; but the number from these sources was comparatively so insignificant that a consideration of them may be omitted. A proposition was even entertained of making servants of the women sent over for wives, whether they married or not.

residents in the colony also sold themselves into servitude for various reasons. The demand for servants before the rise of slavery was always very great in the American colonies and was further enhanced by that of the island plantations. It was the impossibility of supplying this by the regular means that furnished the justification professed in the English penal statutes[1] and gave encouragement to the illicit practice of spiriting. In the early years before these means were resorted to, dealing in servants had become a very profitable business. The London merchants were not slow to see the advantages of such a trade; a servant might be transported at a cost of from £6 to £8 and sold for £40 or £60, and a systematic speculation in servants was begun both in England and in Virginia.[2] Regular agencies were established, and servants might be had by any one who wished to import them " at a day's warning."[3] Others were consigned to merchants in Virginia or sent with shiploads of goods on a venture.[4] The demand continued unabated till near the last quarter of the seventeenth century. The numbers were so considerable in 1651 that the Commissioners of the Commonwealth who were sent to demand the submission of Virginia were authorized, in case of resistance, to levy the servants for reducing the colony.[5] From this time to the beginning of the decline of the system the yearly importations were very large, the number imported from 1664 to 1671 averaging 1500 a year.

---

[1] Hening, III., 449; 4 Geo., c. 11, etc.

[2] Append. to Eighth Rept., etc., 41; Cal. State Papers, Col. 36, 76, 77, 100; Smith, II., 105; Purchas, His Pilgrimage, p. 1787.

[3] Verney Papers, Camden Soc. Pub.; Neill, Virginia Carl. 109.

[4] Cal. State Papers, Col. 36, 258, 268.

[5] " New Description of Virginia," London, 1649; Thurloe State Papers, Vol. I., 198. The general muster of 1624 shows the number of servants then in Virginia as 378 in a population of 2500. They were well distributed, most of the planters having but one or two. Afterwards many planters brought in as many as 30, and in 1671 the servants were 6000, 15 per cent. of the population. Hening, II., 515.

Several causes combined to fasten the system very early upon Virginia: the stimulus given to the acquisition of wealth resulting from the establishment of private property in land;[1] the phenomenally rapid growth of tobacco culture, occasioned by the productiveness of labor employed in it, and the returns to be had in ready money from its sale;[2] the increasing cost of hired labor; the "head right" of fifty acres which was received for every person transported;[3] but particularly the unfortunate condition of the laboring classes in England, whose real wages (owing to the great rise in prices in the latter part of the sixteenth century) were exceedingly low and gave rise to a large class of unemployed.[4]

Legal Status of the Servant.—The history of the legal development of the institution properly begins with 1619 and falls broadly into three general periods:

First, 1619-1642, characterized by the development of certain incidents of servitude from practices originating in the first twelve years of the Company's government. These gradually become fixed during this period chiefly in Customary Law.

Second, 1642-1726, in which the incidents of the former period are extended and further established by Statute Law,

---

[1] Col. Rec. Va., Declaration, etc. The ancient planters regarded the massacre of 1622 as a judgment on their greed.

[2] The tobacco culture was introduced into Virginia by Governor Yeardley in 1616, and even in this year restrictions had to be imposed to prevent the planters from altogether neglecting corn. In 1619, Secretary John Pory tells us that their "riches consist in Tobacco," and their "principall wealth" in servants, "but they are chargeable," he says, "to be furnished with armes, apparel and bedding and for their transportation and casuall both at sea and for their first yeare commonly at lande also, but if they escape they prove very hardy and sound able men." Purchas, His Pilgrimage, 837, Rolf's Relation; Campbell, 117; Pory to Carleton, Mass. Hist. Soc., IX., 4th, 9, 10.

[3] Smith, 165; Mass. Hist. Coll., Vol. IX., 4th sec., p. 10, note. See Pory to Carleton; Va. Co. of London, Va. Hist. Coll., Vol. VII.; Vol. I., 14, 15.

[4] Cunningham, 201, 422. Purchas, His Pilgrimage, p. 1821.

and the system reduced to legal uniformity in contrast to the somewhat varying practices of the courts in the former period. The institution reaches also in this period its highest practical development.

Third, 1726-1788, the period of decline of the system in consequence of the rising institution of negro slavery.

First Period, 1619-1642.—After the Assembly of 1619, until near the middle of the century, very little direct legislation appears in regard to servants, but in this interim there grew up many customs recognized by the tribunals which affected very seriously the personal rights of servants. One of the earliest and most important customs was the right assumed by the master to assign his servant's contract whether he gave his consent or not. This originated in the practice with the Company of disposing of apprentices and servants to planters on their agreeing to reimburse the Company for the expenses of the servant's transportation, and in the custom with officers of the government of renting their tenants and apprentices to planters in order to insure an easier or more certain support. The depressed condition of the colony following the Indian massacre of 1622 made the sale of servants a very common practice among both officers and planters.[1] In 1623 George Sandys, the treasurer of Virginia, was forced to sell the only remaining eleven servants of the Company for mere lack of provisions to support them, and a planter sold the seven men on his plantation for a hundred and fifty pounds of tobacco. The practice was loudly condemned in England and bitterly resented on the part of servants, but the planters found their justification in the exigencies of the occasion, and their legal right to make the sale seems never to have been actually called into question.[2] Assignments of contracts for the

---

[1] Neill, London Co., 356, 375; Append., 8th Rept. Com. on Hist. MSS., 6, 39; Cal. S. P., Col. 36.

[2] App. 8th Rep., I. and III., 39, 41-44; Smith, Hist., II., 40; Va. Hist. Mag., Oct., 1893, 162. The servants wrote indignant letters to their friends. One says he was "sold like a d——

whole or the unexpired portion of the servant's term became from this time forward very common. As a result the idea of the contract and of the legal personality of the servant was gradually lost sight of in the disposition to regard him as a chattel and a part of the personal estate of his master, which might be treated and disposed of very much in the same way as the rest of the estate. He became thus rated in inventories of estates, and was disposed of both by will and by deed along with the rest of the property.[1]

But aside from these incidents of property which attached to the condition of the servant, his position before the law was very little different from that of the freemen of the colony. His personality was recognized by the enactment of special laws for his protection and in his being subjected, with the rest of the colonists, to the payment of a poll tax for the support of the government and of tithes to the minister. In the early period, like a freeman, he was liable to military service in behalf of the state. He enjoyed rights of trade, except with the Indians, and could acquire property. His testimony was always received in court, unless he was a convict, and he was a valid witness to contracts.[2] His religious instruction was provided for in the same manner as that of freemen. The courts carefully guarded his contract and effected speedy redress of his grievances. He might sue and be sued, and had the right of appeal to the supreme judiciary of the colony, and throughout this period he enjoyed the important political right of the suffrage on an equality with freemen, a right which in most cases had not been exer-

---

slave," but admits that his master's whole household "was like to be starved." Rolf says the "buying and selling of men and boies or to be set over from one to another for a yearly rent or that the tenants or lawful servants should be abridged their contracts" was held "a thing most intolerable in England."

[1] Accomac Rec. MS., 61, 82 (1635); Robinson MS., 9; York Co. Rec., 86.

[2] Hening, I., 123, 143, 144, 157, 196.

I

cised before.[1] In penal legislation, however, the distinction was generally made between the servant and the freeman in the servant's liability to corporal punishment for offenses for which a freeman was punished by fine or imprisonment. A law of 1619 provided that " if a servant wilfully neglect his master's commands he shall suffer bodily punishment," but the right of the master to regulate his servant's conduct in this way was of slow growth and had no legislative sanction before 1662. During this period correction remained in the hands of the Assembly and of the courts.[2]

When Wyatt came as Governor in 1621 he was instructed to see that all servants fared alike in the colony and that punishment for their offenses should be service to the colony in public works, and by a law of 1619 servitude for wages was provided as a penalty for all " idlers and renegates."[3] That such provisions should be realized it was necessary for the servant to perform service in addition to the term of his contract. In this we have the germ of additions of time, a practice which later became the occasion of a very serious abuse of the servant's rights by the addition of terms altogether incommensurate with the offenses for which they were imposed. It became a means with the courts of enforcing specific performance of the servant's contract, and was so applied contrary to the common law doctrine relating to contracts, which only provided for damages in cases of breach of contract and not for specific performance.[4]

The common law of England had the character of national law in the colony, and accompanied the colonists as a personal law having territorial extent. Although the relation of master and servant in the case of apprenticeship as an extension of the relation of parent and child, guardian and ward, was an effect of the common law having personal

---

[1] *Ibid.*, 150, 157, 330, 333, 334, 403, 411, 412 (also 217); Acc. Rec. MS., 2,' 24, 54, 76, 84; Col. Rec. Va. Laws, 1619.

[2] Col. Rec. Va., 1619, 25, 28; Hening, I., 127, 130, 192.

[3] Col. Rec. Va., 12 *et seq.*; Hening, I., 117.

[4] Robinson MS., 52.

extent, yet the relation of master and servant in indented servitude was unknown to that law, and could neither be derived from nor regulated by its principles. It had to depend entirely for its sanction on special local statutes, or on the action of tribunals which had no precedents before them and acted as the necessities of the occasion demanded, with little regard to established doctrines of the common law. The growth of the institution is thus marked by the development of local customary and statute law, and only very gradually assumed a fixed shape as this development proceeded.[1]

The master's title to service rested on the provisions of the contract. These were very varied, sometimes specifying, besides the ordinary conditions, treatment of a special nature, sometimes stipulating for a trusteeship of such property as the servant possessed, and sometimes for gifts of land or of apparel and corn sufficient to set the servant up as a freeman when his term had expired.[2] Such provisions were recognized by the courts in their strict enforcement of the contract, and led to the establishment of customary rights such as additions of time and freedom dues. A servant might claim on the expiration of his term freedom dues in apparel and corn whether stipulated for or not. Their amount was at first customary and determined where sued for by appointees of the court, but finally they became fixed in statutory law.[3]

Monthly courts were held as early as 1622, and by virtue of their general jurisdiction over all cases not involving more than a hundred pounds of tobacco (which was later extended to £5 and £10 causes and to those of less than 1600 pounds of tobacco) they had jurisdiction over disputes between master and servant within this limit, and the Commissioners as conservators of the peace had power to regulate the conduct

---

[1] Hurd, Law of Freedom and Bondage, I., 116, 129, 139, 210, 220; Reeves, Eng. Law, II., 598; Anson, Law of Contract, 213 sq.
[2] Acc. Rec. MS., 88 (1637); Essex Rec. MS., 140 (1686).
[3] Hening, I., 303, 319, 346; II., 66, 70. Rob. MS., 8; Acc. Rec. I., 10, 272, 273, 519; II., 58, 68; MS. Rec. Genl. Ct., 158; Col. Rec. Va., 81.

of the servant whenever necessary. Before this the Governor and Council or the General Assembly had had sole jurisdiction of all causes. After quarter courts were established in 1632 appeals lay to it, as before to the Governor and Council, and to the Assembly as the supreme appellate court in the colony. The servant by his right of suit in these courts and of appeal had a speedy and effective remedy for his grievances, and the rulings of the justices established many precedents which greatly mitigated the conditions of his servitude.[1] The judges when they were acquainted with the English law at all put a most liberal construction upon it and generally in favor of the servant. In breaches of contract *discharge* was often granted for insufficient reasons, and for misusage or non-fulfilment of any of the conditions by the master, the servant, if he did not obtain his freedom, might have his term lessened and be granted damages. The courts also often enjoined such action on the part of the master as would repair the injuries sustained by the servant. In 1640 a master who had bought a maid-servant, "with intent to marry her," was ordered by the General Court to do so within ten days or to free her on the payment of 500 lbs. of tobacco. And where insufficient food and clothing

---

[1] In 1643 the ten monthly courts were reduced to six County Courts, with jurisdiction over cases above 20 shillings, or 200 lbs. of tobacco. Cases of less amount could be decided in the discretion of any commissioner. The inconvenience of resorting to the general court at Jamestown caused a grant in 1645 of general jurisdiction of all cases in law and equity to the county courts. Two years later the jurisdiction of the General Court was limited to cases of 1600 lbs. of tobacco in value or over. In 1662 there were 17 county courts having jurisdiction in all cases " of what value or nature whatsoever not touching life or member," and the name Commissioner was changed to Justice of the Peace. The Quarter Courts now became the General Court, held twice a year, and appeals lay to it as formerly, and from it to the Assembly. In 1659 appeal to the Assembly had been limited to cases involving more than 2500 lbs. of tobacco. This limitation was removed in 1661, and justice facilitated by a reference of all cases except those of the winter term to itinerant chancellors.

were provided servants were taken away until the master corrected the fault.[1] When the record of his contract was not sufficient to protect the servant on the expiration of his term from the greed of his master, he might make it appear upon testimony in the County Court that the conditions of the contract had been fulfilled and receive a certificate of the fact, which thus became indisputable evidence of his right to freedom. The courts also recognized the servant's right to acquire and hold property.[2]

In the practices of the courts regulating the punishment of servants we see the way prepared for later provisions of the statute law not so favorable to them. By virtue of the power of the courts to regulate the private as well as the public conduct of servants, and by the discretionary power given by enactments to the Governor and Council, they might be subjected to indignities of punishment not worthy of a freeman. In but few cases did the courts permit servants' offenses to be punished by fine; the usual penalty was whipping or additional servitude to the master or to the colony. This probably would not have been the case if the servant had generally had anything wherewith to discharge a fine, but as he had not, some other means of satisfaction was found necessary. Penal legislation regarding servants did not differ greatly in severity, however, from that applied to freemen, except in the case of absconding servants, where very severe punishment was early inflicted, designed by its severity to prevent recurrence of the offense.[3] Towards the

---

[1] Rob. MS., 8, 9, 27, 68, 243 sq.; Acc. Rec., 2, 39, 44, 58, 76, 35, 45, 85, 86, 91, 82. In 1637 a bad character, John Leech, threatened to have his master " up to James City to see if he could not get free of a year's service," alleging " that his master had not used him so well as he formerly had done," and that he would use against him speeches made by the master against the Governor and Council.

[2] Rob. MS., 8, 9, 68; Acc. Rec., 35, 76, 82.

[3] Robinson MS., 9-13, 27, 66, 69; Acc. Rec., 107. A number of servants, for a conspiracy " to run out of the colony and enticing divers others to be actors in the same conspiracy," were

end of the period the servant's great abuse of his rights of trade, by allowing himself to be tempted by loose persons to embezzle and sell his master's goods, made necessary some restriction. The Assembly of 1639 conditioned this right henceforth on the master's consent, imposing severe penalties upon persons who should induce any servant to trade secretly, and the courts seem to have rigidly enforced the provisions of this act.[1]

Before the close of the first half of the century, then, we have seen the growth, mainly through judicial decisions, of certain customary rights on the part both of the servant and of the master as recognized incidents of the condition of servitude. These were on the part of the servant the right to a certificate of freedom, to freedom dues and to the possession of property; on the part of the master, to the free assignment of the servant's contract by deed or will, to additions of time in lieu of damages for breach of contract, and the right of forbidding the servant to engage in trade. Corporal punishment and additions of time have also become the ordinary modes of regulating the servant's conduct and punishing his offenses.

Second Period, 1642-1726.—From the year 1642 the statute books begin to fill with legislation concerning servants, mainly confirming or modifying such rights as had been already developed and subjecting the system of servitude to more uniform regulation. Until 1643 no definite term had been fixed by law for the duration of servitude when not expressed in indentures. The terms specified in the indentures varied from two to eight years, the usual

---

to be severely whipped and to serve the colony for a period of seven years in irons. This was in 1640. "Saml. Powell for purloining a pair of breeches and other things from the house of Capt. Jno. Howe deed. shall pay ffower dayes work to Elias Taylor with all charges of the court and the sheriff's ffees and to sit in the stockes on the next Sabbath day with a ribell in his hatt from the beginning of morninge prayer until the end of the sermon with a pair of breeches about his neck."

[1] Hening, I., 275, 445; Robinson MS., 10, 17 (1640).

one being from four to five years, but until this time custom had regulated the servitude of such persons as came in without indentures, and what was known as servitude "according to the custom of the country" had begun to grow up. Where no contract but a verbal one existed there was always room for controversy between master and servant, each trying to prove an agreement that would be to his advantage. To put a stop to such controversies the Assembly passed a law definitely fixing the term in all cases where servants were imported "having no indentures or covenants," according to the age of the servant. The master was at first the judge of the servant's age, but as this naturally worked to the servant's disadvantage, the judgment of ages was put in the hands of the county courts after 1657. Unless the master produced his servant in court for this purpose within four months after arrival he could only claim the least term allowed by the law, and after 1705 the servant had two months allowed in which to prove an alleged indenture for a less time.[1]

By the beginning of the period several abuses had grown up that prevented or seriously interfered with the master's realization of his right to service. Hitherto there had been no legal restriction to prevent a man-servant from marrying, though by an act of 1619 a female servant could not marry without the consent either of her parents or of her master, or of both the magistrate and minister of the place, upon pain of severe censure by the Governor and Council. The right of free marriage was one which for very obvious reasons would work to the disadvantage and inconvenience of the master, particularly if the marriage was made without his knowledge, and in 1643 a law was passed providing "that what man servant soever hath since January 1640 or hereafter shall secretly marry with any maid or woman servant without the consent of her master he or they so offending shall in the first place serve out his or their tyme or tymes

---

[1] Hening, I., 257, 411, 441; II., 169, 297, 447.

with his or their masters—and after serve his master one complete year more for such offence committed," and the maid " shall for her offence double the tyme of service with her master or mistress." When the offender was a free man he had to pay double the value of the maid's service to her master and a fine of 500 lbs. of tobacco to the parish. For the offense of fornication with a maid-servant the guilty man was required to give her master a year's service for the loss of her time, or, if a freeman, he might make a money satisfaction. In 1662 the master's losses from neglect of work or stolen goods and provisions were sufficient to make necessary a further restriction upon the secret marriage of servants. The act provided that " noe minister either publish the banns or celebrate the contract of marriage between any servants unless he have from *both their masters* a certificate that it is done with their consent," under penalty of the heavy fine of ten thousand pounds of tobacco. Servants, whether male or female, guilty of marriage contrary to the act, with each other or with free persons, suffered the addition of a year's time to their servitude, and the guilty free person was condemned to a like term of service or the payment of 1500 lbs. of tobacco to the master.[1]

Another great abuse was the practice which greedy and wealthy planters had of covenanting with runaway servants as hirelings or sharers on remote plantations, thus encouraging them by more favorable terms to desert their proper service. This had been anticipated by an enactment of the Assembly of 1619, which provided " that no crafty or advantageous be suffered to be put in practice for inticing away tenants or servants of any particular plantation from the place where they are seated," and that it should be the " duty of the Governor and Counsell of Estate most severely to punish both the seducers and the seduced and to return them to their former places." But by 1643 the practice on the part of these planters had become so flagrant that com-

---

[1] Col. Rec. Va., 28; Hening, I., 253, 438; II., 114; III., 444.

plaints of it were made at every quarter court, and the Assembly enacted that any person so contracting with a servant and entertaining him for a whole year, without a certificate of the freedom of the servant from the commander or commissioner of the place, should forfeit to the master twenty pounds of tobacco for every night the servant was entertained, while the servant was to be punished at the discretion of the Governor and Council.[1]

But more than anything else the habit on the part of servants themselves of absconding from their masters' service, stealing their masters' goods and enticing others to go with them, worked to the detriment of the masters and the peril of the colony. The courts had attempted by the most severe punishments to put a stop to the practice. Whipping, additions of time from one to seven years, branding, and even servitude in irons, proved ineffectual. The possibility of entire escape from servitude or of service on better terms proved too great a temptation, and with an unruly class of servants such attempts became habitual. Statute after statute was passed regulating the punishment and providing for the pursuit and recapture of runaways; but although laws gradually became severer and finally made no distinction in treatment between runaway servants and slaves, it was impossible to entirely put a stop to the habit so long as the system itself lasted. The loss to the master was often serious even if he recovered the servant. A loss of time from several months to a year or more, and the expense of recapture, which at first fell upon him, made the pursuit of the servant often not worth while for the remaining time for which he was entitled to his service.[2] The rise of this practice was not due to the severity of the service to which the servant was subjected. The courts, we have seen, provided a speedy remedy for any misusage, and by an act of 1642 it was provided that " where any servants shall have just cause

---

[1] Col. Rec. Va., 22; Hening, I., 253, 254, 401.
[2] MS. Rec. Genl. Ct., 201; Hening, III., 277, 452, 458.

I

of complaint against their masters or mistresses by harsh or unchristianlike usage or otherwise for want of diet, or convenient necessaryes that then it shall be lawful for any such servant or servants to repair to the next commissioner to make his or their complaint." The commissioner was then required to summon the master or mistress before the county court which had discretion to settle the matter, taking care "that no such servant or servants be misused by their masters or mistresses where they shall find the cause of the complaint to be just." Runaways began to increase with the importation of an undesirable class of servants, a few of whom were present in the colony from the earliest days, and who during this period were largely recruited by the addition of felons and "spirited" persons. They were 'the common offenders, and by their habits corrupted the better class of servants.[1] When this class grew more numerous in the latter half of the seventeenth century servants became so demoralized that they would run away in "troops," enticing the negro slaves to go with them. In counties whose situation made escape peculiarly easy the abuse was very great. In 1661 it had become so bad in Gloucester that the Assembly authorized that county to make whatsoever laws it saw fit to meet the case of such runaways.[2] Servants would plot how they might run away even before they landed in Virginia,[3] and under the liberty given them on the plantations, and with an accessible back country, it was not a difficult matter to accomplish. They frequently made their escape to the adjoining provinces of Maryland and North Carolina, where their condition being unknown they might enjoy their freedom, or if discovered their recovery was attended with such difficulties as to insure their safety.

---

[1] MS. Rec. Va. Co., Library of Congress, II., 21; Westover MSS., II., 240. Cal. State Papers, Col. 19: Domestic, 447, 594, 1635, July 8, Dec. 5. Purchas, His Pilgrimage, 1809 (Virginia Verges); Neill, Lond. Co., 120, 160, note.

[2] Hening, II., 273.   [3] *Ibid.*, III., 35.

The right of the master to claim his servant in another jurisdiction was one not always recognized, even though the institution existed there, as it depended on colonial legislation having an intercolonial application. In the absence of statutes providing for the return of fugitive servants from one jurisdiction to another, the justices refused to take the responsibility of acting, and so frequently much injustice and inconvenience resulted. The only redress left to the master was the power to levy on goods in Virginia belonging to inhabitants of the province in question.[1] North Carolina became such an asylum for absconding servants and slaves that it was popularly known in Virginia as the "Refuge of Runaways." The Eastern Shores of Virginia and Maryland were also favorite resorts. Servants frequently escaped to the Dutch plantations and sometimes even to New England. To restrict the practice and to prevent absconding debtors, a pass was required for any person leaving the colony, and masters of ships were put under severe penalties not to transport any servant or slave without such a pass or license from his master.[2] Certificates of freedom were also required to be given in due form to every servant on the expiration of his term, and under the power given by the statutes any person travelling in the colony, if not able to give an intelligent account of himself or to show his certificate, might be taken up as a runaway. The law for the capture of runaways was at first very inefficient, and went through a number of experimental changes before one that was effective was discovered. In the first acts relating to runaways no

---

[1] Hening, I., 539; Northampton Rec., II., 149; Hening, 1661, Drummond's servant. An interesting question might have arisen as to the master's claim had a runaway servant escaped to England or to a foreign country where the institution was not recognized. No such case seems to have occurred. A transported felon would probably have been seized and treated as an escaped convict in England, but what remedy the master could have had in this case, or when the fugitive was not a felon, is not clear.

[2] Hening, III., 271; IV., 173; IX., 187.

means of discovery and no method of pursuit and return to the master were prescribed. The pursuit seems at first to have devolved upon the master, but the loss resulting from this caused the General Court in 1640 to direct pursuit to be made by the sheriff and his posse at the expense of the county from which the fugitive escaped. Pursuit by hue and cry, adopted from the English custom, seems also to have been in use, but by 1658 it had been so much neglected that a special act for its enforcement was necessary.[1] Constables also pursued under search-warrants, but they neglected their duty, and in 1661 the Assembly had to promise them rewards of 200 lbs. of tobacco from the master. This proved insufficient and had to be increased and even paid out of the public revenues, to be reimbursed by the master. Additional rewards from £3 to £10, according to the value of the servant and his distance from home, were offered by masters. In 1669 the practice was so bad that any one was permitted to take up a runaway and receive a reward of 1000 lbs. of tobacco from the public, to be reimbursed by the servitude of the offender " to the country when free of his master."[2]

In consequence of the growth of these abuses, and designed as a corrective of them, we find a great extension of the principles of additions of time and of corporal punishment, to such a degree in fact as to prove often a source of great injustice to the servant. The principle of additions of time, we have seen, was early extended by the action of the

[1] Hening, I., 255, 401, 483, 539. Reeves, V., 355 (rev. ed.). The hue and cry was an ancient method of pursuing offenders in England, and rested on the statute of Winchester, 13 Edward I., 81, 82, c. I., and on 28 Ed. III., c. II. In Virginia a warrant was issued by the governor or some of the council, or a commissioner of the county, and masters of households were put under penalty of 100 lbs. of tobacco for its speedy conveyance from house to house.

[2] Hening, II., 21, 273; Va. Gazettes, 1736, Dec. 17, Feb. 25, Mar. 11. To facilitate discovery, habitual runaways had their hair cut " close above the ears," or were " branded in the cheek with the letter R." Hening, I., 254, 440, 517.

courts beyond its application as a punishment merely, and became the ultimate resort of the master in his legal claim of damages for breaches of contract by the servant;[1] but some confusion seems to have existed in the minds of the judges and the framers of the later statute law as to the exact theory on which the principle should be applied. Though continued as a punishment until the abolition in 1643 of servitude to the colony for offenses, it seemed in the case of several kinds of offenses, both before and after that time, to partake of the nature of damages to the master for loss resulting from the offense, as well as of a penalty for the offense itself. In other cases it was clearly viewed in the light of damages alone. It was of the former character generally in such offenses as secret marriage and fornication, and of the latter for unlawful absence from his master's service or for acts of violence toward his master or overseer. The term of servitude that was imposed was determined by the offense or the damage sustained, and was, except in a few offenses, not excessive, varying from one to two years.

---

[1] MS. Rec. of Genl. Ct., 1640, 3, 8, 9, 10, 11, 12, 13, 16, 52, 53; Acc. Rec. MS., 1633, 10. The practice of the courts was not uniform, however. The General Court, on the 9th of July, 1640, ordered two runaway servants to be punished by whipping and "to serve out their time and add a year to their master to recompense his loss by their absence"; but a few months later a master was denied his claim to three months service due him by a servant's loss of time. At a court held the following week, the master of certain runaways is given a year's additional service, or "longer if said master shall see cause" for their loss of time, and for sheriff's fees paid by masters, "the servants shall make good the same at the expiration of their time by a year's service apiece to their said masters." A maid-servant who was guilty of fornication was ordered to "serve her full time to her master as by covenant," and her husband to make satisfaction "for such further damages" as the master should make appear. The Accomac county court ordered a servant "to perform the full term of his indentures faithfully and truly" or to stand to the "censure" of the court. This was a case where recourse might have been had on the freedom dues as damages, but the court left these to the servant.

In such cases as fornication or having a bastard the addition might be considerable. A woman-servant, for having a bastard, served her master from one and a half to two and a half years, and if the bastard were by a negro or a mulatto she might be sold to additional service for five years for the benefit of the public. Besides the master's claim on the female servant he might claim also a year's service from the guilty man, but in both cases the servant was given liberty to discharge this claim by a money satisfaction as in the case of free persons.[1]

The greatest abuse of additions, however, arose in connection with runaway servants. Before terms were definitely specified by statutes they were capable of very arbitrary assessment at the hands of the courts. The length of the term was sometimes left to the discretion of the master or was adjudged more than he himself cared to exact. Additional terms from two to seven years, served in irons, to the public, were prescribed in extreme cases.[2] The additions possible under the statutes were also very great, as ultimate recourse was had on the servant for all the expenses of his capture and return to his master. These expenses included rewards, sheriff's fees and jail fees. These latter were not fixed until 1726, and were a source of great abuse. When the master refused to pay these expenses, or could not be found, the servant was publicly sold or rented for such a time as would repay the public disbursements, and was then returned to his master to serve the remainder of his time and that due by addition.[3] The act of 1643 provided that runaways from their " master's service shall be lyable to make satisfaction by service at the end of their tymes by indenture (vizt.) double the tyme of service soe neglected, and in some cases more if the commissioners—find it requisite and con-

---

[1] Hening, I., 438; II., 114, 115, 168; III., 87, 140, 452. By an act or 1662 the father was liable to make satisfaction to the parish by additional service for the keeping of the child.

[2] Robinson MS., 9-13; MS. Rec. Genl. Ct., 154, 161.

[3] Hening, I., 255, 539.

venient," and subsequent acts allowed the master to recompense himself by service for all expenses to which he had been put in recovering his servant. The rate at which he could do this was fixed by the act of 1705 at one year's service for every 800 lbs. of tobacco, or a month and a half for a hundred pounds.[1] The servant, however, might commute this penalty by giving security for the payment of these expenses within six months, and the master was forced to accept security or payment when offered. The servant was also protected from injustice by the necessity imposed upon the master of presenting his claim in the next county court after the return of the runaway, or becoming liable to the loss of it altogether.[2] Where the master's goods had been stolen, or negroes enticed to accompany the runaway, the addition of time sufficient for compensation might be large. The servant was required to serve for the lost time of the negro as for his own, since the negro was held by a statute of 1661 to be "incapable of making satisfaction by addition of time."[3] Additions thus frequently amounted to as much as four or five years, or even seven in some cases, and were often more than the original term of servitude.[4]

Corporal punishment as a common mode of regulating the servant's conduct was acquired by the master as a legal right during this period, and when retained in the hands of the local magistrate or other officers it became, under the power given by the statutes, readily susceptible of abuse. The extension of this important power beyond the administration of the courts was largely a result of the necessity of providing some severe correction in the case of runaways.

[1] Hening, II., 458.

[2] *Ibid.*, III., 456, 458, 459; IV., 168, 171; XII., 191.

[3] *Ibid.*, II., 26. This is said to be the first statute sanctioning negro slavery in Virginia, but as early as 1625 the status of the negro, according to Jefferson, was determined by a case in the General Court. Jeff. Cases, Genl. Ct., 1730, etc., 119, note.

[4] MS. Rec. Genl. Ct., 1672, 3, 12, 15, 35, 44, 154, 158, 161, 188.

I

The servant had generally no means wherewith to remit a fine, and so in penal offenses, where free persons were fined, we have seen that the servant was whipped, unless his master discharged the fine. In many cases also it was a general punishment both under the laws of England and under those of the colony, so that a law of 1662 provided for the erecting of a whipping-post in every county; but even before this time the master had assumed the right of administering corporal punishment to his servant. In this year it became a right recognized by law, but when a master received an addition of time for his servant's offense it remained doubtful whether corporal punishment could also be administered. This question was settled by the Assembly in 1668. It was declared that " moderate corporal punishment " might be given to runaways either by the master or by a magistrate, and that it should " not deprive the master of the satisfaction allowed by law, the one being as necessary to reclayme them from perishing in that idle course as the other is just to repair the damages sustained by the master."[1] The power thus given was doubtless abused, for in 1705 an act was passed restraining masters from giving " immoderate correction," and requiring an order from a justice of the peace for the whipping of " a christian white servant naked," under penalty of a forfeit of forty shillings to the party injured. The act is significant as showing also the master's right to employ corporal punishment as a regulation of the conduct of servants in general.[2]

Slaves were for the first time included in the act against runaways in 1670, and it was provided " that every constable into whose hands the said (fugitive shall by any commissioner's warrant be first committed shall be and hereby is enjoyed by vertue of this act (though omitted in the warrant) to whip them severely and convey him to the next constable (toward his master's home) who is to give him the like correction and soe every constable through whose precincts

<hr />

[1] Hening, II., 75, 115, 118, 266.   [2] *Ibid.*, III., 448.

he passeth to doe the like.'"[1] In 1705 the severity of this act
was somewhat mitigated by requiring justices who made the
commitment to the constable to specify in their warrants the
number of lashes to be given the runaway, "not exceeding
the number thirty nine." Corporal punishment was also
extended in offenses committed against the master solely.
In 1673 the General Court ordered that a servant "for scan-
dalous false and abusive language against his master have
thirty nine lashes publicly and well laid on in James City and
that he appear at Middlesex County Court next and there
openly upon his knees in the said court ask forgiveness
which being done is to take of any further punishment allotted him."[2]

Besides the power to regulate his servant's conduct and enforce the performance of his duties, the master acquired a
sort of general control over his servant's person and liberty of action. By custom the servant enjoyed frequent
respites from service and might freely employ this time as he
saw fit. In consequence of an abuse of this privilege, however, it became necessary to restrict it upon the consent of
his master. The plot of certain servants in Gloucester
county in 1663 to rise against their masters and subvert the
government caused great alarm throughout the colony, and
led to a strict regulation of the liberty previously allowed servants of leaving their masters' plantations and assembling
together. To suppress "unlawful meetings of servants," an
act directed "that all masters of ffamilies be enjoyned to
take especial care that their servants do not depart from their
houses on Sundays or any other dayes without particular
lycence from them," and the different counties also were
empowered to make by-laws for preventing unlawful meetings and for punishing offenders.[3]

---

[1] Hening, II., 278.   [2] MS. Rec. Genl. Ct., 44, 136.
[3] Hening, II., 195; cf. 171, 441; Neill, Va. Carolorum, 295,
296. Beverley, 55, 56. The attempt was made by a number of
transported Oliverian criminals, who made use of the general
political and religious discontent of the time. It was not a servile
insurrection due to the harsh treatment of servants.

Though the servant's right to the personal enjoyment of his property was recognized when protected by the terms of his contract or by the courts, his disposal of it became conditioned on his master's consent by the acts against dealing with servants, and the right of trade was practically taken away.[1] The habit had also grown up on the part of masters of converting to their own use goods brought in by their servants or afterwards consigned to them. In 1662 an act was passed to restrain this, providing that all servants "shall have the propriety in their owne goods and by permission of their master dispose of the same to their future advantage." The revisal of 1705 confirmed the right of servants to goods and money acquired "by gift or any other lawful ways or means," with "the sole use and benefit thereof to themselves," making no reference to the necessity of the master's consent for a disposal of them. The continuation of the act against dealing with servants was a practical limitation, however, of any rights they may have had.[2] The servant's right to the possession of his personal estate now rested on statute and not on the occasional action of the courts or the will of his master; but he could not during servitude acquire a freehold interest in land, and tenancy of small tracts with the permission of the master was exceptional.[3]

Other important rights became fixed or limited by

---

[1] Hening, I., 274, 445; II., 119.

[2] Hening, II., 165; III., 450, 451; IV., 49. The servant frequently enjoyed the right of trade, however, with his master's consent, and many masters, besides paying wages or making gifts of money and stock, allowed servants the use of tracts of land. (Bullock, Account of Va., 1649, 52, 59.)

[3] Hening, IV., 46, 47, 49. An act of 1713 restrained a servant and overseer from keeping horses "without the license in writing of his master or mistress," nor could the master give license for the keeping of more than one, the reason by the act alleged being that great numbers were kept by persons who had no interest in land, and were so "suffered to go at large on the lands of other persons," which was "prejudicial to the breed of horses" and "injurious to the stocks of cattle and sheep."

the statute law of the period and certain new rights were developed. The servant's claim to freedom dues recognized by the custom of the country and enforced by the courts was at first only a general one and not specific, the amount granted varying according to the will of the master or of the court in which it was sued for, unless it had been specified in the contract. A clause was inserted in the act of 1705 confirming this right and making it thereafter certain in amount. Every male servant was to receive upon his freedom " ten bushels of indian corn, thirty shillings in money or the value thereof in goods and one well fixed musket or fuzee of the value of twenty shillings at least "; a woman-servant, fifteen bushels of Indian corn and forty shillings in money or value. In later times these dues were discharged by a money equivalent and gifts of apparel.[1]

The freedom of a servant could be proved either by reference to the registry of his contract or to a court record, if he did not himself have a certificate of the fact from the county court or commissioner or from his master. In 1662, to facilitate the discovery of runaways and to protect innocent persons from arrest as such, or from penalties for entertaining suspected runaways, the clerk of the county court was directed to issue a certificate of freedom to every servant who adduced proof before the court of the expiration of his term.[2] Though designed as much for the protection of the master as of the servant, it became of great importance to the latter as his title to liberty and a guarantee that his rights as a free man would be fully respected. The necessity of such a guarantee appears not only from the restrictive nature of the legislation of this period, but from the records of the old General Court. Meager as they are, they present a number of instances of servants suing for their freedom who were either held or sold for periods longer than their lawful time.[3] The right was much abused, however, on the part of

---

[1] Hening, III., 151.   [2] Hening, I., 254; II., 116.
[3] MS. Rec. Genl. Ct., 150, 156, 158, 161, 162, 166, 173, 204, 218 (1673-75).

the servant. Heavy penalties had continually to be inflicted to prevent the theft of certificates or the use of forged or counterfeit ones. Stringent regulations had to be put on the granting and re-issuing of them, and where the servant made a fresh contract for service the certificate was to remain in the hands of the master till the contract expired.[1] The servant was further protected from an involuntary extension of his contract with his master by any intimidation or pressure brought to bear upon him by reason of his unequal position. After 1677 no contracts for further service or for freedom dues could be made by a master with his servant during servitude except with the approbation of " one or more justices of the peace," under penalty of having to free his servant. By 1705 any contract for " further service or any other matter relating to liberty or personal profit " between master and servant had to be made in the presence and with the approbation of the court of the county. A practical limitation was also put upon the master's absolute right of assignment of his servant's contract. As the white servant was considered a Christian, as originally from a Christian land, the principle was established that he could only be held in servitude by Christians or those who were sure to give him " christian care and usage." Thus free negroes, mulattoes or Indians, although Christians, were incapacitated from holding white servants, and so also were all infidels, such as " Jews, Moors and Mohometans." Where any white servant was sold to them, or his owner had intermarried with them, the servant became " ipso facto " free.[2]

An important right acquired by the servant during this period was the power given him to bring his complaint into court by petition " without the formal process of an action." This right, confirmed by the act of 1705, proved a great boon to the servant in case of unjust usage. The county court had full discretion in such a case and might free or sell

---

[1] Hening, I., 254; II., 116; III., 454, 455.
[2] Hening, III., 450.

the servant away from his master. The right was extended to complaints of every character affecting the servant's rights. He could in this way sue for his freedom dues, his property or wages, or for damages for unlawful whipping. Another right granted by the act was that of commutation by a money satisfaction of corporal punishment for breach of the penal laws, and of additions of time for the expenses of capture in the case of runaways.[1] A right which was implied, if not expressly stipulated for in the contract, was that of a sick or disabled servant to claim support and medical attention at his master's charge during servitude, without any reciprocal right on the part of the master to further service therefor. The master was prevented by the liability of his goods and chattels to seizure from avoiding this obligation by freeing his servant and throwing him upon the parish.[2]

Such rigor as is perceptible in the legislation of this period, and in general regarding the servant, we have seen appears particularly in the case of runaways, and is to be traced to the influence of the developing institution of slavery. Little practical distinction was made in the treatment of runaway servants and slaves where the practice was habitual, and the servant by his association with the negro fugitive became subjected to indignities that would not otherwise have been inflicted.[3] The influence of slavery is also to be traced in the disposition to regard the servant as property and subject to the same property rights as the rest of the personal estate. As an important part of his master's estate he had become liable to the satisfaction of his debts and could be levied on equally with the goods and chattels.[4]

---

[1] Hening, III., 448, 452, 453, 459.   [2] *Ibid.*, III.; 449, 450.
[3] *Ibid.*, III., 456; IV., 170, 171.
[4] Northampton Co. Rec., 147, 149; Fitzhugh's Letters, July 22, 1689. Fitzhugh writes to Mr. Michael Hayward that his debtor's estate is probably sufficient to save his debt, as he has "4 good slaves with some other English servants, and a large stock of tobacco"; York Co. Rec., 86.

The conception of the servant as a portion of the personal estate is shown to be fully developed by an act of 1711, which directed that servants and slaves should be continued on the plantation of a person who died intestate, or who did not otherwise direct in his will, to finish the crop, upon which they were to remain in the hands of the executors or administrators; while the slaves were then to pass to the heirs at law, as by the act of 1705 they had been declared to be real estate.[1]

The period is thus characterized by a twofold development: first, on the part of the master, from a conception of his right to the service guaranteed by the contract and to such incidents as enabled him to realize this right, to a conception of property in the servant himself which he would employ to the utmost advantage allowed him by the law; and on the part of the servant, from a desire to fulfil the conditions of his contract to a desire in general to escape from servitude whether based on lawful contract or on the exaction of his master: secondly, a reduction of the relation of master and servant to fixity and uniformity throughout the colony by the action of statute law in ascertaining their respective rights and duties.

Third Period, 1726-1788.—During this period the institution of white servitude gradually declined before the growing institution of negro slavery, which proved economically far superior to it. We find the development of no new rights on the part of the master, and on the part of the servant only that of assent to the assignment of his contract. This was not granted until 1785, when the system itself was practically at an end. The contract could now be assigned only on the free consent of the servant, attested in writing by a justice of the peace.

The various modifications introduced affecting rights already established were generally in mitigation of the servant's condition, and point to a very rapid decline of in-

---

[1] Hening, IV., 284.

dented servitude after the middle of the century. This is indicated by a reduction of penalties for such abuses as harboring runaways or dealing with servants, and by the repeal in 1763 of former acts providing for the servitude of persons who came in without indentures, while making no provision to regulate it in future. In 1765 the practice of binding the bastard children of a white woman-servant or free woman for thirty-one years was declared by the Assembly to be "an unreasonable severity to such children," and the term was limited to twenty-one years for males and eighteen for females. By the act of 1769 they were to be treated as apprentices, to be instructed and to claim all the rights of other apprentices.[1] Unimportant changes were introduced in the law relating to runaways designed to facilitate their recovery with least expense to the master and consequently with least injustice to the servant.[2] Freedom dues were fixed with a money equivalent, and were the same for both men and women. Injury to a servant might be redressed by "immediate discharge" from service by order of a court. The legislation as a whole was not important and developed no new principles. The legal fixity of the conception of the servant as a piece of property is apparent, and becomes further developed through the influence of slavery and as a result of the long terms, of from seven to fourteen years, on which the English felons were transported to the colony.[3]

The act of 1785 legally defines servants as "all white persons not being citizens of any of the confederated states of America who shall come into this commonwealth under contract to serve another in any trade or occupation." This definition excluded slaves, hirelings who were citizens of any of the confederated states, but included convicts (whose importation was not finally prohibited until 1788) and apprentices from abroad. The term of servitude was limited

---

[1] Hening, III., 445, 451; V., 552; VI., 359, 360; VIII., 134, 135, 136, 337.

[2] Hening, V., 552, 557; VI., 363; VIII., 135, 136.

[3] Hening, XII., 150, 151, 191; 6 Geo. III., c. 32; 8 Geo. III., c. 15.

to a period not exceeding seven years, except in the case of infants under fourteen who might be bound by their guardians until the age of twenty-one, and all servants, the act declares, " shall be compellable to perform such contract *specifically* during the term thereof." Corporal punishment by order of a justice was the power in a master's hands of enforcing such performance, and the benefit of the servant's contract was to pass to " the executors, administrators, and legatees of the master." [1]

We have seen that the relation of master and servant was at first a relation between legal persons, based on contract, and that such property right as existed consisted in the master's right to the labor and services of his servant, while the servant enjoyed a reciprocal right to support and, to some extent, to protection and instruction from his master; that gradually the conception of property grew at the expense of that of personality, and that with a limited class of servants personal liberty became so restricted that they stood in respect to their masters in a position somewhat analogous to that of slaves. The broadest practical and legal distinction was made, however, between the servant in general and the slave, and the institution of white servitude differed widely from that of slavery, both in nature and in origin. It rested for its sanction on national or municipal law alone, while slavery was based upon international as well as municipal law. In extent servitude was of limited duration, while slavery was for life. The personality of the servant was always recognized and his status could not descend to his offspring, as was the case with the slave's, nor did the master at any time have absolute control over the person and liberty of his servant as of his slave. The servant always had rights which his master was bound to respect, and besides the guarantee of personal security enjoyed a limited right to private

---

[1] Hening, XII., 190, 191; *Ibid.*, Justice, 417, 418; Hening, XII., 668.

property. The conception of the servant himself as a piece of property did not go beyond that of personalty, while the slave did not remain as personal estate, but came to be regarded as a chattel real or as real estate. The mutual effects of the institutions upon each other are shown, however, in the growth of this conception of property, and particularly also in the legislation respecting runaways, unlawful assemblies, or absence from the master's plantation. Servitude may thus be regarded as preparing the way both legally and practically for the institution of slavery as it existed in Virginia.[1]

Social Status of the Servant.—The actual condition of the servant, though in great measure determined by his legal status and by certain social laws, was also largely influenced by many customs that had no sanction in law, and the distinction between servant and slave became as clearly defined under the action of these and the practical working of the law as in the letter of the law.

In regard to employment a marked distinction was frequently made between the servant and the slave. The industry of the colony was chiefly agricultural, its staple

---

[1] Hurd, Law of Freedom and Bondage, I., 116, 129, 139, 210, 220. Robinson MS., 10, 243, 250, 256, 261. This is shown in the application of corporal punishment and of additions of time, and in the disposition to claim negro and Indian servants as slaves. In 1640 the addition of time for a negro runaway servant was, in a case brought before the General Court, servitude "for the time of his natural life here or elsewhere." Hening, II., 118, 288, 481; III., 277; IV., 168, 171, 174, 202; Va. Gazettes, 1737; Tucker's Blackstone, Appd., 55-63. Though slavery assumed a comparatively mild form in Virginia, much of the criminal law relating to slaves was of a very discriminating and harsh character, as was also the procedure. Cf. acts of 1723, 1748, 1764, 1772; Minor, Institutes, I., 161 et sq. Until 1772 no restriction was put on the outlawry of a slave, he might be killed in resisting arrest, and until 1788 the murder or manslaughter of a slave by his master might go unpunished, the presumption being that he would not wantonly destroy his own property.

The influence of servitude upon slavery will be discussed at greater length in a monograph on Slavery in Virginia, now in preparation.

throughout the seventeenth century being tobacco. Where the servant was engaged in field labor he was worked side by side with the negro slave, under the direction of overseers who were frequently the best of his own class. This was not in itself a hardship, as the work was the same as that of the planters themselves and of every common freeman, and the servant was not required to do more in a day than was done by his overseer. As the number of negroes began to increase, the harder and greater part of the work was put upon them, and the servant, as more intelligent, was reserved for lighter and finer tasks. Though associated with the negro, he was not compelled to live with him in " gangs " and " quarters," and, unlike him, could make complaint if insufficient clothing or lodging were provided.[1] Women-servants were commonly employed as domestics, as by an act of 1662 they became " tythable " and their master subject to the payment of levies for them if they were put "to work in the ground "; the negress, however, had no such exemption in her favor and was frequently employed in field labor with the men. With regard to their labor, the slave, Beverley says, was better off than the husbandmen and day-laborers of England, and the servant's lot was still easier. Very large numbers of the servants were also artisans and skilled workmen and were employed in building and other trades. Almost every profession was represented, and on the large plantations, which provided mostly their own necessities, there was a great demand for such servants and for industrial apprentices. Many servants were thus taken into the families of their masters in various capacities, and were treated with as much consideration as if working under a free contract for wages. Considerable domestic manufacturing was of necessity carried on at all

---

[1] Va. MS. B. R. O., 302; Jones, Present State, 36.

[2] Beverley, 219; Jones, Present State, 37; Hening, II., 170; Fitzhugh, MS. Letters, Jan. 30, 1686-87; Force, III., L. and R., 12.

times, and after the introduction of large numbers of slaves for the field labor, white servants were generally utilized for that purpose. They were thus better housed, clothed and fed than the negro, as a result of the position they occupied toward their master as well as from the protection afforded them by the law.[1]

Besides a general social obligation of protection and defense recognized by most masters toward their servants as dependents, the law only held a servant responsible for his own free acts and not for those performed under the orders of his master.[2] Where the servants were apprentices a high personal trust was involved, and the master, besides occupying the position of guardian, was bound to render religious and secular as well as mechanical instruction. Not only was attendance at church required by law, but all servants and apprentices were to be instructed together with their masters' children every Sunday "just before evening prayer" by the minister of the parish. When such obligations were recognized, the great distinction between the positions of a servant and a slave is at once manifest.[3] Where these obligations rested upon the provisions of the contract they seem to have been carefully guarded by the courts. A servant complained in a general court of 1640 of her "master's ill usage by putting her to beat at the mortar for all his household" when he had promised "to use her more like his child than a servant," and to teach her to read and instruct her in religion, and the court considering the "grevious and tyran-

---

[1] Carpenters, joiners, sawyers, bricklayers, blacksmiths, engravers, weavers, shoemakers, tailors, saddlers, bakers, teachers, surgeons and other craftsmen were imported. Va. Gazettes, 1736 sq.

[2] Col. Rec. Va. Laws, 1619, 21, 28; Winder MSS., I., 245 (1667); Hening, III., 462, 463; IV., 425.

[3] *Ibid.*, I., 143, 144, 157; II., 260; III., 459; IV., 133; XII., 681; Jones, 92, 94; Stat. at Large Va., III., 124. Before 1667 baptism had in many cases been refused to slaves and their offspring, since doubts existed as to its effect on their status. It was then settled that baptism did not free the slave.

ical usage" of her master, ordered her to be freed, though she had yet a year to serve, and to receive her freedom dues.[1]

Frequent respites from service were also granted. It was not only the custom to allow servants Saturday afternoons as well as the Sabbath for free disposal, but all the old holidays were rigidly observed. An industrious servant was thus given an opportunity to lay up a competence for his start in the world as a free man. Tenure of small tracts of land was sometimes permitted by masters, and with the live stock given him he might raise cattle, hogs and tobacco and so become possessed of considerable property. The evolution from the days of the London Company of an aristocracy of wealth rather than of blood was a somewhat slow process, so that there was nothing in the servant's position itself (except that it debarred him from the possession of landed property and consequently of certain civic rights) to condemn him to a very inferior social position. No odium attached to his condition or person as to the slave's, and where he proved worthy of consideration he might enjoy many of the social privileges that would have been accorded him as a free man.[2]

The servant himself was disposed to regard his condition as only that of a free man rendering services for a sort of wages advanced to him in his transportation and maintenance, and his legal disabilities as only a temporary suspension of his rights necessary to insure a more complete realization by his master of the right to service. Constantly looking forward to his full freedom, he considered his position as analogous to apprenticeship, or to that of the ordinary hired laborer rather than to that of the slave. The natural pride of the free man sustained by this feeling, together with the strong race prejudice that has ever separated

---

[1] Robinson MS., 8.

[2] Force, III., L. and R., 14; *Ibid.*, Virginia's Cure, 7, 10; Bullock, 52 sq. Instances are related of their appearing at social gatherings in their masters' houses on equal footing with the family and their guests.

the Englishman from an inferior and dependent race, and his
religious sentiment as a Christian, or at least of Christian
origin, sufficed to make a very great practical distinction
between his social position and that of the negro and Indian,
slave or free.   These sentiments were effective with the better class of servants in keeping them aloof from association
with such inferiors.   With convicts and the lower classes,
where such considerations were not always sufficient, the
law took precaution by the most stringent measures to up-
hold them and to prevent race contamination.   Freemen
and servants alike were subjected to severe penalties for
intercourse with negroes, mulattoes and Indians, and intermarriage with them or with infidels was prohibited by many
statutes prescribing the punishment both of the offender
and of the minister who performed the ceremony.[1]   The

[1] Hening, I., 146, 552; II., 170; III., 86, 252. The Governor and
Council in court in 1630 ordered " Hugh Davis to be soundly
whipped before an assembly of negroes and others for abusing
himself to the dishonor of God and shame of a christian by de-
filing his body in lying with a negro which fault he is to
acknowledge next sabbath day." A similar case came before
the court the next year. Very few negroes, however, were
brought to Virginia before the latter half of the century, but
the records of the general court during the period (1670-76) of
increased importations of negroes under the African Company,
having no reference to the recurrence of the offence, points to
a disposition on the part of the whites in general to avoid race
contamination. The growth of a considerable class of mulattoes,
particularly mulattoes by negroes, is appreciable towards the
end of the century, however, and is shown by the passing of
several acts to restrict it. The first statute on the subject, that
of 1662, imposed double fines for fornication with a negro,
but no occasion for restricting intermarriage seems to have
arisen till 1691, when an act was passed " for prevention of
that abominable mixture and spurious issue which hereafter
may encrease in this dominion as well by negroes, mulattoes
and Indians intermarrying with English or other white women
as by their unlawful accompanying with one another," and punished the intermarriage of a free white man or woman with a
negro, mulatto or Indian, bond or free, with banishment forever from the colony within three months after the marriage,
and the justices of the county were " to make it their perticular
care that this act be put into effectual execution." The revisal

limitation of servants' marriages upon the master's consent was a sufficient safeguard in their case, and but little responsibility may be regarded as attaching to them for the growth of the mulatto class. As was natural between two dependent classes whose conditions were different and widely in favor of one class, race prejudice and pride were at their strongest and developed jealousies which did not exist between the master and his dependent or the freeman and the slave. A disposition on the part of servants to keep themselves free from all association with negroes is very perceptible.

The presence in the latter part of the seventeenth century of quite a number of the English lower classes and criminals, together with a greater development of the aristocratic sentiment from the influx of a considerable number of gentlemen just after the civil war in England,[1] had the effect of les-

---

of 1705 altered this penalty to the imprisonment of the offender six months and a fine of ten pounds Virginia currency, the person who performed the marriage forfeiting ten thousand lbs. of tobacco. When a woman-servant was guilty of having a mulatto or negro bastard she was, as a free woman, sold for five years as a punishment, or subjected to a fine of fifteen pounds, while the necessity of the master's license barred the unlawful intermarriage of servants. Where the offense occurred, then it was more likely to do so in the case of a free person than of a servant, as the master would not be likely to give his consent to any such marriage, having much to lose and nothing to gain from the service of the issue which might be sold away from him by the churchwardens of the parish. In one instance a girl was given her freedom because her master had consented to such a marriage, and such rulings of the courts probably checked exceptional cases. The practical distinction to be made between servants as whites, and negroes and Indians was one constantly recognized by the courts and the Assembly. The consideration of racial distinction alone seems to have led the Assembly in 1670, when the question of the legal power of the free Christian Indian or negro to hold a servant came up, to declare in the negative. Hening, II., 168, 280; III., 86, 87, 453, 454; Rob. MS., 256.

[1] Beverley, 232, 233; Wirt, Life of Henry, 34. Va. MSS. B. R. O., Vol. II., pt. I., 291. The importance of the introduction of these persons into Virginia society has been probably exaggerated. Gov. Nicholson, writing to the Lords of Trade, Dec. 2, 1701, says: " Fit and proper persons for executing the several

sening the barrier between servant and slave and increasing that between the ruling and dependent classes. Yet with the middle classes, the smaller planters and the yeomanry, who still constituted the great body of the inhabitants, and were to an important extent recruited from the freed servants themselves, no such caste feeling was produced, and the general social position of the servant continued to be widely distinguished from that of the slave.

The real condition of the servant in the American colonies was much better than has generally been supposed, and was decidedly better in Virginia than in some of the other colonies. Though what was practically white slavery seems to have existed in some of the island plantations of England, there is no instance, so far as I have been able to discover, of a white person sold into slavery in Virginia. How far the general character of white servitude differed from slavery has been sufficiently shown, and in considering the apparent barbarities to which a servant was subjected we should remember that neither in England nor on the Continent was the condition of the dependent classes any better. The doctrine of the rights of man had not yet arisen in the seventeenth century, nor was it until the latter part of the next century that its practical fruits began to appear. It was reserved for the revolutionary movement of the eighteenth and nineteenth centuries, which brought political and re-

offices and imployments decrease—in twenty or thirty years if the natives cannot be prepared fewer or none will be found capable of executing the several offices, for there is little or no encouragement for men of any tolerable parts to come hither, formerly there was good convenient land to be taken up and there were widdows had pretty good fortunes which were encouragements for men of good parts to come but now all or most of these good lands are taken up and if there be any widdows or maids of any fortune the natives for the most part get them, for they begin to have an aversion to others calling them strangers. In the civil war several gentlemen of quality fled hither and others of good parts but they are all dead, and I hope in God there never will be such a cause to make any come in again." Beverley, who was opposed to Nicholson and his government, confirms this view.

I

I

ligious liberty to America and a great part of Europe, to completely develop the idea of personal liberty. Not until the late years of the eighteenth century was feudal serfdom generally abolished on the continent of Europe, and as late as 1835 the prison and the flogging board still constituted a part of the equipment of every Hungarian manor.[1] In England villeinage passed away comparatively early as a result of the social disturbances of the fourteenth century, though a case was pleaded in the courts as late as 1618. Its extinction was thus gradual without any legislative abolition, and it was many years before the principle of free contract labor was fully worked out. The tendency of the agrarian reforms of England, in contrast to those of some continental countries, was to develop a class of landless freemen whose position was worse than if they had possessed land on semi-servile conditions. The small farmer gradually gave way before the capitalist farmer, and the large laboring class that was formed was stripped of all interest in the soil. These laborers were compelled to work by the various statutes regulating labor and apprenticeship under some master, and had to do so generally on long terms, with fixed wages and hours of labor, and restrictions were placed on departure or dismissal from service under severe penalties. The system introduced by the final statute of laborers, the so-called Statute of Apprentices of 1563, embodying the results of many previous measures, had the effect of checking migration of servants and in general of lengthening the period of servitude, and remained effective until the industrial revolution which followed the introduction of machinery.[2]

Some improvement in the economic condition of English servants is discernible during the latter part of the seventeenth century, but not much can be said as to the betterment of the social condition. Where they were in their master's household, and received rations and apparel in part pay-

[1] Fyffe, Mod. Europe, I., 21, 24, 26.
[2] Taswell-Langmead. Constitutional History of Eng., 316, note; Cunningham, 40-42, 184, note, 192, 198-200, 362, 387, 388.

ment of wages, they were not generally as well fed and clothed as the indented servants in Virginia. Their labor was more burdensome and the arbitrary treatment to which they were subjected was frequently more severe. Corporal punishment was a common mode of regulating their conduct, and shackles were used to prevent their running away. For extreme maltreatment on the part of the master the only redress was discharge from service, or in some cases a paltry forfeit of less than a pound to the servant. They were frequently discharged from their service contrary to the statute, and besides maltreatment their wages and apparel were often withheld. The condition of the English servant was thus sufficiently bad to make numbers of them migrate to Virginia in the hope of bettering it.[1]

---

[1] Cunningham, 192, 193, 196; Beverley, 220; Jones, 92. Oldmixon, 290: "If hard work and hard living," he says, "are signs of slavery, the day laborers in England are much greater slaves." Middlesex Co. Rec., II., 22, 100, 101, 120, 130, 138; III., 23, 117, 318; *Ibid.,* S. P. Rolls, Oct. 8, 1655; *Ibid.,* 6 Chas. I., p. 34; 18 Chas. I., 117; 13 Chas. II., 318; Aug. 27, 1652, p. 209; 4 Chas. I., 23. The Middlesex records and sessions rolls give a number of interesting cases that throw light on the condition of the English servant. For an assault upon his master, an offense which would have been punished in Virginia by whipping or addition of time, a servant was in 1618 adjudged "to be imprisoned for a year, to be flogged on two market days at Brainford, to be put one day in the stock at Acton and on his knees in the open church to ask forgiveness of his master and afterwards to be reimprisoned." Unruly and disorderly servants and apprentices were sent to houses of correction, when they became effective after 1609, "to labour hardlye as the quality of their offence requireth." In 1652 a servant on covenant for a year's service complained of her mistress, and the sessions found "that the said lady did violently beat her servant with a great stick and offered to strike her with a hammer and that the said lady doth retain the wages due," and ordered dismissal and payment. In another case a master confesses "that he hath most uncivilly and inhumanly beaten a female servant— with great knotted whipcord—so that the poor servant is a lamentable spectacle to behold." Another master was held to answer "for giving his servant immoderate correction by beating him with three roddes one after the other." A case which must be regarded as very exceptional occurred in 1655. An ap-

That the servant sometimes met with very harsh treatment cannot be denied, however. In a case of judicial punishment by a commissioner of a county court, before the punishment had been regulated by statute, a servant was whipped almost to death, and the passing of an act by the Assembly in 1662 prohibiting private burial of servants or others, because of the occasion thus given for "much scandall against divers persons and sometimes not undeservedly of being guilty of their deaths," shows that sometimes the master abused his right of corporal punishment in an extreme degree.[1] The cruelty of some masters was sufficient towards the middle of the seventeenth century to interfere seriously with the importation of servants, and the Assembly in 1662 attempted to put a stop to it by giving the servant an easy remedy upon complaint to the commissioners for all his grievances. From this time forward harsh treatment may generally be considered as exceptional. Beverley says of the treatment of servants, "The cruelties and severities imputed to that country are an unjust reflection, no people more abhor the thought of such usage than the Virginians nor try more to prevent it now whatever it was in former days." This statement seems to be borne out by other contemporary authorities and by the records of the courts, which show that every safeguard was thrown around the servant, and that wherever the slightest pretext for freeing him appeared it was taken advantage of. Justice was readily accessible. Every few miles a justice might be found to whom complaint could be made, and the county courts, which met in

---

prentice complained that his master made him work on Sunday and further misused him "by fastening a lock with a chain to it and tying and fettering him to the shoppe and that said master, his wife and mother did most cruelly and inhumanly beat his said apprentice and also whipped him till he was very bloody and his flesh rawe over a great part of his body, and then salted him and held him naked to the fire being so salted to add to his pain."

[1] Acc. Rec., 80; Hening, II., 35, 53. In 1661 the Assembly confirmed an order of the General Court forbidding a man and his wife "to keep any maid servant for the term of three years."

the early times as often as necessity required, and later every
month, redressed servants' grievances in a " summary " manner.[1]

A servant could legally sue for his freedom on retention
in service after his contract had expired, or for his master's
violation of the act of 1676 by attempting to make any contract with him to his damage, or upon purchase by negroes,
mulattoes, Indians or infidels, or upon the intermarriage of
any such person with his owner; but the courts going beyond this in the discretionary power granted them by law,
would free a servant for breach of the terms of indenture by
the master, for breach of a contract to marry, for a second
complaint of ill usage, and sometimes even upon a first com-

---

[1] Force, I., L. and R., 4; Hening, I., 435; II., 117, 118, 129, 488;
Beverley, 219, 220, 222; cf. Bullock, Jones, Virginia's Cure, Leah
and Rachel, pp. 11, 12, 15-17. John Hammond in 1659 warns
servants against mariners, shipmasters and others who imported
them merely for gain, and advises them to covenant for liberty,
to choose their own master and a fortnight's time after their
arrival in which to do so, "for ye cannot imagine," he says,
" but there are as well bad services as good but I shall shew ye
if any happen into the hands of such crooked dispositions how
to order them and ease yourselves when I come to treat of the
justice of the country which by this they may prevent." From
this traffic in servants by middlemen it is evident that much
deception and fraud might be practiced upon the unwitting,
both before and after reaching Virginia. They were deceived
in making their contracts by such general stipulations as for
an allotment of land "according to the custom of the country,"
which was represented to them as being 50 acres, when no allotment to the servant was customary at all until after 1690.
False indentures seem to have been made also, either through
corruption in the registry office or by forgery, as a number of
blank indentures, properly signed and sealed, were brought to
the notice of the Assembly in 1680, and all judgment of their
validity, when alleged, was lodged in the discretion of the justices. The practice of selling men on shipboard to the highest
bidder, or of consigning them to merchants at Jamestown or
other ports for sale, might, of course, result very unhappily for
servants, and during the voyage to Virginia they often suffered
great hardships for want of clothes, bedding and diet. These
were mild, however, compared to the "horrors of the middle
passage " in the days of slavery.

plaint where no fault of the servant appeared. The number of such suits occurring both in the General and the county courts, and the fraudulent concealment of indentures, show a continual disposition on the part of the master to extend the servitude, though unjustly, for as long a period as possible.[1] By the acts giving the master additions of time for the birth of a bastard child to his servant a premium was actually put upon immorality, and there appear to have been masters base enough to take advantage of it. This was restrained by an act of 1662, which provided that the maid-servant should be sold away from her master in such cases and no compensation allowed him for the loss of her time. Complete freedom would probably have been granted but for the harmful effect on the servant herself.[2]

The speedy rendering of justice to the servant through the special procedure provided in his case, and the unrestricted right of appeal to the higher courts, placed him in an exceptional position. The fact that the law was interpreted in the most favorable light possible for the servant, and that no fear was ever entertained of a servile insurrection, except in the single case of the Gloucester plot of 1663, which was due to political rather than social reasons, may be regarded as confirming the positive statements of contemporary writers as to the comparatively easy conditions of servitude during the

---

[1] Hening, II., 280, 388; III., 447; IV., 133; MS. Rec. Genl. Ct., 159, 162, 166, 173, 204, 218, 238; Robinson MS., 2, 8, 256, 265; Gen. Ct., 154, 156, 158, 161; MS. Rec. Va. Co., III., 233, 292; Acc. Rec., 2; Essex Rec., 132; Henrico Rec., 85; Force, III., L. and R., 16. Verbal agreements were sometimes alleged, and where proven, or where the servant could not produce his indenture, they might be enforced. An indenture, however, was an effectual bar to any such agreement.

[2] Hening, II., 167; III., 453; MS. Rec. Genl. Ct., 8. The number of false pleas brought into court by servants to get a reduction of their time, and the offenses of which they appear to have been guilty, show that the master was more likely to be imposed on than the servant. Genl. Ct., 8, 12, 15, 44, 47, 158, 188, 1675, Oct. 2; Acc. Rec., 85; Henrico Rec., 41; Robinson MS., 27.

period of indented service. We may conclude that where the servant showed himself at all deserving his lot was in general very easy and frequently much better than he had ever before enjoyed.[1]

---

[1] Except in the early period and in 1777, the servant was free from the obligation of military service, and, as in the case of slaves, the law did not allow the sale of spirituous liquors to them. Hening, III., 400; VI., 74; VII., 93, 101; IX., 32, 81, 271, 275, 592; Sparks' Washington, Vol. II., 168, 169.

CHAPTER III.

THE FREEDMAN.

We have seen that by provisions of the statutes and under the practice of the courts a servant might legally obtain his freedom in several ways; the ordinary mode, however, was on the expiration of the term of his contract. He might then claim a certificate of freedom, and with his title to liberty resting on this or on the records of a court, all his legal disabilities were at once removed and he became " as free in all respects and as much entitled to the liberties and privileges of the country as any of the inhabitants or natives."[1]

To determine the place and influence of the servant as a freedman in the very complex social and economic development of the colony is by no means an easy matter. Merged as he was in the general class of free men, such effects as were due to his presence were not easily distinguishable. The process itself was largely unconscious on the part of the people and but barely recorded in contemporary history. Little historic material has thus survived on which to base satisfactory conclusions. Enough remains, however, to give decisive proof of a very rapid evolution of servants when free, and to show that they did not continue as a class at all, and so could not have formed, as has been mistakenly supposed, the lowest stratum of Virginia society in the eighteenth century. The various classes that made up the society of colonial Virginia were separated from each other only by the broadest and most general distinctions, and graded almost imperceptibly into one another. The law recognized no distinction whatever except in the case of the

---

[1] Beverley, 220 sq.

twelve councillors. The class which stood at the head of the social order and formed a kind of aristocracy was mainly an outgrowth of the official class and of landed proprietors, who, having acquired wealth or large estates, had been able to preserve them in their families for several generations through the action of the law of entails. A number of wealthy would-be aristocrats, without real culture and refinement, together with the poor but proud younger sons of the aristocrats, hung on to and aped the manners of the class above them; but the solid middle class of independent yeomanry, with plain and unpretentious manners, was far more numerous, and even in the latter part of the eighteenth century formed nearly half the population of the colony. The lowest class of all is described by a contemporary as "a seculum of beings called overseers, the most abject, degraded, unprincipled race."[1]

The freed servants may in all justice be said to have recruited all these classes at different periods during the continuance of indented servitude, but toward the beginning and in the first years of the eighteenth century probably more largely that of the small independent planters or laborers and the class of overseers. Though pride and wealth generally acted to make the upper classes hold themselves aloof from the lower, the good-will and generous hospitality characteristic of all classes gave them all more or less of a common life and freedom of association with each other, and where those elements were present in any man that would merit his rise he was not likely to be kept down by any false ideas due to caste sentiment. The rapidity with which some freedmen rose to positions of trust and distinction is abundant proof of the opportunity which lay open to all that possessed true desert. Many servants were besides this of better origin and education than the generality of freemen, and were frequently employed in such respon-

[1] Wirt, Life of Patrick Henry, 33, 36; *Id.*, British Spy, 192-194; Anbury, Travels through the interior parts of America, London, 1789, 371-376.

sible positions as teachers, and many ministers were imported on conditions almost parallel to those of indented servants.[1]

In the first half of the seventeenth century their rise to prominence was often very rapid. Several members of the Assembly of 1654 were men who had been servants, and in 1662 we are told that "the Burgesses which represent the people . . . are usually such as went over servants thither," who "by time and industry . . . have acquired competent estates."[2] Intermarriage of free persons and servants was very common. Masters sometimes bought female servants for their wives, and it was not uncommon for men-servants to marry into their masters' families when they gained their freedom.[3] No impassible social barrier thus seems to have

---

[1] Col. William Preston, of Smithville, Va., bought at Williamsburg, about 1776, a gentleman named Palfrenan, as a teacher for his family; he was a poet and a scholar, a correspondent and a friend of the celebrated Miss Carter, the poetess, and also of Dr. Saml. Johnson. This man educated many of the Prestons and Breckenridges in Virginia and Arkansas. The distinguished Wm. C. Preston of S. C. was one of his pupils. Richmond Standard, June 9, 1880, Letter of Mrs. Floyd; Va. Hist. Mag., Oct., 1894, p. 236, Will of Col. John Carter (1669).

[2] Neill, Va. Car. 279. 290; Force, III., Virginia's Cure, 16; Howe, 207. Peter Francisco, a Revolutionary soldier celebrated for his personal strength, had been an indented servant for seven years. "He was a companionable man and an ever welcome visitor in the first families in this region of the state," says a contemporary living in Buckingham County. Cf. "A Declaration," etc., 4, 57; York Rec., 1633-34; Rob. MS., 52; Col. MS., 17.

[3] Rob. MS., June 3, 1640; Wm. Byrd's Letters, June 9, 1691; Bullock, 52 sq. Bullock advises English fathers to send their daughters to Virginia rather than their sons, and promises that they "will receive instead of give portions for them." "Maid servants," he says, "of good honest stock may choose their husbands out of the better sort of people. Have sent over many but never could keep one at my plantation three months except a poor filly wench made fit to foille to set of beauty and yet a proper young fellow served twelve months for her." He tells men-servants how they may prosper by their service and lay up a competence, "and then," he says, "if he look to God, he may see himself fit to wed a good man's daughter." Bullock was a Yorkshireman and had had seven years' experience in Virginia when he wrote in 1649. Cf. McDonald, II., 68.

existed, nor were opportunities lacking for the material improvement of the servant. To better his fortune when out of indenture at least two courses were open to him. He might remain with his master or some other person as a hired man or tenant upon his lands, or he might become an independent planter by taking up whatever unoccupied land in the community had proved too barren to be already patented by freemen, or by moving to the frontier where abundance of good land was to be had on the easiest terms.

There was a constant demand for labor, both agricultural and mechanical, throughout the colonial period, a demand satisfied neither by the indented servants nor by the large importations of slaves. The wages of hired labor were consequently always high, particularly those of artisans or tradesmen of the slightest capacity. Freedmen who were content to become members of the laboring class had abundant opportunity and inducement to do so. Until domestic manufacturers were checked by the repressive measures of the English Board of Trade, considerable encouragement was given to skilled workmen to exercise their crafts or to establish themselves in an independent position. When the profits of tobacco-planting increased, however, this industry probably absorbed a large number of freedmen, as very favorable conditions of tenantship were offered on the great estates, where men usually held on what constituted practically a life tenure. The disposition to become a freeholder, however, particularly after the servant enjoyed a claim to land in his own right, was most marked of all.[1] In the

---

[1] Acc. Rec., 36, 37, 42; Va. MS. B. R. O., V., pt. 2, pp. 302, 317, 336, 386, Nov. 11, 1708, Nov. 29, 1728; Robinson MS., 180; Bullock, 62 sq.; Beverley, 225; Hening, I., 208. 301; II., 172, 472, 503; III., 16, 30, 50, 53, 75, 81, 108, 121, 187, 197. Large importations of craftsmen had been made by the planters without satisfying their needs, and men were specially encouraged to remain in the employ of their former masters or to serve the community in their trade. Many servants received in addition to their transportation and support, wages equal to those paid the best servants in England. Though the colony was chiefly agricultural in character

earlier times, though the person importing him could claim fifty acres for his importation, the servant does not appear to have been legally entitled to any grant of land from the government. A grant was frequently stipulated in the contract with a master, and became also in some places a custom, which like freedom dues was recognized by the courts. In 1690 the instructions to Governor Howard directed that every servant receive a patent of fifty acres in fee on attaining his freedom, and it is probable that henceforth he was regarded as having a legal claim to such a grant. Before this the rules for leasing or patenting lands in many cases allowed him to acquire the tenancy of small tracts at a nominal rent, and lands were also left with other bequests to ser-

and dependent on England for many of the ordinary articles of manufacture well into the eighteenth century, it is a great mistake to suppose that no manufacturing or attempts to build up trade appeared in Virginia. The fact that attempts were not largely successful was due not to domestic causes alone, but to the policy of the English Board of Trade, whose interest it was to keep Virginia agricultural for the benefit resulting to English commerce. The repeated efforts of the Assemblies to develop manufactures and to crush out the slave trade were defeated in England rather than in Virginia. In the late years of the seventeenth century and early years of the eighteenth, the difficulty of obtaining goods from England and the low price of tobacco gave the planters excuse for establishing considerable manufactories on their plantations; cotton, woolen and linen goods were made, and shoemaking and tanning were undertaken on a somewhat large scale. These industries grew to such an extent that great fear was aroused among English merchants of the loss of a very profitable part of their trade. The letters of the Lords of Trade are full of questions in regard to this new departure, and of recommendations and instructions to discourage it as much as possible. In 1707 as many as four counties on the south side of James river were given over to the production and manufacture of such goods, and a considerable trade had sprung up with New England and the islands. The Lords recommended the Queen the next year, from fear of a great loss to her revenues, to appoint a fleet and a convoy to sail from England every year with all such commodities as the planters needed, to prevent their applying their labor to any other product than tobacco. Exports of corn, pork and " great cattle" were made from Virginia to New England as early as 1639. Rob. MS., 180.

vants in their masters' wills.[1] The practice of the sale of rights to land due for the importation of people, to the colony, both by the holders of them and by the secretary, for the small sum of four or five shillings, and the modes of granting out lapsed and escheated lands, made it a very easy matter in later times for the servant to become the proprietor of landed property[2] in the old settled communities,

[1] Va. MSS. B. R. O., 318; *Ibid.*, II., pt. I., 81 (1698); Henrico Rec., 36; Hening, I., 161, 209; Rob. MS., 57, 61. In 1626 much of the common land that had belonged to the London Co. was leased to the large number of tenants and servants, then freed, in such quantity and for such a number of years as seemed necessary, at the yearly rent of one pound of tobacco per acre. Cf. McD. MS., I., 295.

[2] Beverley, 220, 226, 227; MS. Rec. Va. Co., III., 219; Va. MSS. B. R. O., 335, 342; Hening, I., 125, 173, 197, 291, 468; Virginia's Deplorable Condition, 164. Titles to land in the first instance rested on patents granted for special services, for consideration, or for the importation of persons to the colony as settlers. A condition of ceding the land within a limited period after the patent's issue accompanied such grants comparatively early. Where this condition was not fulfilled the land lapsed and a new patent might be issued to any one petitioning the General Court and the Governor, on similar terms, the theory being that land grants were made to encourage settlers only. Seating involved considerable expense for improvements, the building of a house, clearing and planting three acres of every fifty, and a full stocking of the land. All this was more than the patentee to large tracts could undertake. It was not an uncommon thing for the right to land to lapse several times over, unless it could be disposed of by sale. The sale of rights became thus as general as the sale of the land itself, and they were readily purchasable for very small sums. After 1705, fifty-acre rights, according to the Royal Instructions, could be bought at five shillings per right. Escheated lands also, where the escheat was not traversed and no equitable right was shown to the lands, could be easily obtained on petition to the Governor by payment into the treasury of a composition of two pounds of tobacco for each acre. In the early years, however, no time limit was imposed upon the seating of lands, and the abuse of land-grabbing, which had begun almost immediately on the general introduction of property in the soil in 1619, had had sufficient time to result in the concentration of all the best lands along the river-courses in the hands of comparatively few persons. This was facilitated by the ownership or the buying up of large numbers of fifty-acre claims, called "head rights," for the importation of set-

and when good land could not be obtained in this way there was always room for him on the frontier. Though much of the frontier land was patented out in large tracts, to lie unsettled for a time, it was gradually broken up into small ones and disposed of by the owners to squatters and settlers, so that the Piedmont and western parts of Virginia became characterized by farms of moderate extent rather than by large plantations as in Eastern Virginia.[1]

The growth of this class of small farmers was effective in developing over a large portion of the State a very strong type of peasant proprietorship, and sufficiently shows that the servant was under no necessity of becoming either a pauper or a criminal. That he did to some extent recruit these classes is what might naturally be expected from the introduction of English convicts as servants, and after they came in some numbers we have indications that they were responsible for much of the crime committed; but pauperism in Virginia before the first quarter of the eighteenth century was almost unknown.[2]

---

tlers. Claims were admitted for the members of a man's family, himself as well as his wife, children, and all servants imported at his charge, and even for the negroes brought in (this latter kind was soon denied). Corrupt practices prevailed also in the offices issuing the grants, head rights were used many times over, and rights could be purchased of the secretary at three to four shillings, or even a half-crown. In this way large tracts came into the possession of a few men, to lie mostly barren and uncultivated unless tenanted. Tracts of 20,000, 30,000 and 50,000 acres existed of which not fifty were under cultivation. When the two new counties of Spottsylvania and Brunswick were set apart during Spottswood's government, with an exemption from quit-rents for several years, Spottswood himself was accused of taking 40,000 acres.

[1] Hening, IX., 226; Va. MS. B. R. O., May 31, 1721, Spottswood to Lords of Trade; Spottswood's Letters, II., 227. The abolition of the system of entails, which had been stricter in Virginia since 1705 than even that of England, was a further step in this process after 1776 in eastern Virginia also. Spottswood, writing in 1717, says that frontiersmen were generally of the servant class.

[2] Beverley, 223, 258; Jefferson, Works, IX., 255; Jones, 116 sq. The convict class was probably never at any one time very

Under the stimulus of regained freedom and the abundant opportunity afforded for individual endeavor, the freed servant may in general be regarded as growing up with the country, as becoming an independent and often valued citizen, and materially aiding in the development of the resources of the colony. Trained by his long apprenticeship in the best practices of agriculture or of his trade, and thoroughly acclimated, he was better able than a new-comer to take a place profitably both to himself and to the public in the social and political order.

---

large in Virginia, as their importation was discountenanced and every effort made to stop it. Beverley speaks of Virginia as "the best poor man's country in the world—but as they have nobody poor to beggary so they have few that are rich—few ask alms or need them." A testator left five pounds to the poor of his parish, but it was nine years before the executors could find a person poor enough to accept the gift. Where the poor existed, provision was made for them in some planter's family at the public charge.

CONCLUSIONS.

From what has been said the importance of the system of white servitude in colonial development is apparent. Such effects as were due to it were to some extent obscured by the institution of slavery, which, existing for some time alongside the earlier system and finally supplanting it, either greatly counteracted or enhanced its influence. Yet it is possible to make some general deductions as to the social and economic results which followed its introduction into the American colonies. Its superiority to a system of perfectly free labor under colonial conditions could not be doubted if it were certain to lead to the development of a class of independent freeholders. The benefit to production to be derived from long and certain terms of service with contract labor was sufficiently shown in the experience of contemporay England. We can see how advantageously such an extension of the time and certainty of labor supply as was involved in indented servitude, together with the power of control by the master and the economy of providing for large numbers of servants together, would work in a new and sparsely settled country whose industry was chiefly agricultural and dependent for success on a foreign trade and consequently on the efficient management of large landed estates by a capitalist class.[1] Some form of cheap labor was a necessity; the slavery of Christians and white

---

[1] In Virginia and Maryland the existence of such a staple as tobacco, which could only be produced profitably on a large scale and constantly required large quantities of new land, made such a development certain from the first. Tobacco was introduced into Virginia in 1616 and almost immediately became the staple product. The ready adoption of the system in the New England colonies, where such conditions did not exist, however, shows its industrial efficiency.

men was naturally abhorrent, that of Indians impracticable on a large scale, and negro slavery was comparatively slow in becoming an object of desire to the Virginia planters. The gradual and tentative development in practice of indented servitude from what at first was theoretically but a modification of free contract labor clearly shows its recognized economic superiority to such a system as existed in England. Designed not only as a labor supply, but as an immigration agency, it had generally the effect of an industrial apprenticeship, greatly strengthening the position of the capitalist employer and developing a class of industrially efficient free men. It supplied the entire force of skilled and domestic labor of the colony for more than half a century, and continued, after slavery as a general labor supply had supplanted it, to be the source of all high-grade labor well into the eighteenth century. It provided for the growth of a strong yeomanry during the seventeenth and eighteenth centuries, preventing a complete absorption of the land into large estates; and in furnishing a great number of independent settlers and citizens, particularly for the back territory, it had a most marked effect on the political as well as the economic development of the country.[1]

The moral influence of the system cannot in general be said to have been good. The tendency was to harden the master's feeling towards servitude and to prepare him for a more ready adoption of slavery, and the introduction of undesirable classes into a society already lax in habit was not likely to improve the moral tone or the social welfare of the colony.[2]

---

[1] By the temporary disfranchisement of the servant during his term, common after the middle of the seventeenth century, a serious public danger was avoided. There could be no guarantee of the judicious exercise of the suffrage with this class who, for the most part, had never enjoyed the privilege before. Their servitude may be regarded as preparing them for a proper appreciation of suffrage when obtained, and the duties of citizenship. In the later days of public improvement and town-building, the imported craftsmen were a valuable class.

[2] Spottswood Letters, II., 227.

In comparison with the institution of negro slavery, the superiority of white servitude for social and moral considerations seems to have been recognized by the Virginia planters, but from a purely economic point of view its inferiority was fully apparent, and from the first considerable importation of negro slaves the ultimate destruction of the system was easily foreseen. The slowness with which negro slavery was adopted shows a conscious effort on the part of Virginia, so long as it was permitted to act freely, to resist the encroachment upon servitude. At the same time that English policy was forcing[1] slavery upon the colony it cut

---

[1] It is a significant fact that the first negroes were brought to Virginia in 1619, the same year in which the principles of indented servitude may be said to have been fully developed, and yet forty years later there were but three hundred negroes in the colony. From 1664 to 1671 several shiploads of negroes were brought in, and there were two thousand slaves and six thousand servants in Virginia. By 1683 the number of servants was nearly doubled, according to Culpepper, while the negroes numbered only three thousand. (Hening, II., 515; Culpepper's report, Doyle, 383.) From this time servitude gave way before slavery, forced on the colonies by the large importation of negroes by the Royal African Co. under its exclusive charter. It was the policy also of the King and the Duke of York, who stood at the head of the African Co., to hasten the adoption of slavery by enactments cutting off the supply of indented servants. In 1698 the African trade was thrown open to separate traders, and an active competition at once sprang up between them and the African Co., the separate traders making large importations and underselling the Company. Though a law of 1660 gave practical encouragement to the importation of negroes by the Dutch, the colonists had become sufficiently aware of the dangers of slavery in 1699 to lay a discriminating duty upon them for three years, and upon alien servants in favor of the Welsh and English born. The act was continued in 1701, allowing a rebate of three-fourths the duty where the negroes were transported out of the Dominion within six weeks. The duty was continued by the acts of 1704 and 1705 where the duty was laid simply upon "negroes or other slaves." The excuse of revenue was alleged, and brief limitations given to the acts in order to secure their confirmation in England, but the slave traders readily saw that the design was to lay prohibitive duties, and they secured the withholding of the King's assent to as many as thirty-three different acts passed by the Virginia As-

off the supply of indented servants, and the decline of the system after the last quarter of the seventeenth century was very rapid. The final extinction of indented servitude in Virginia did not take place till some time after the close of the Revolutionary War; as late as 1774 there was still some demand for servants,[1] and the importation of convicts was not finally prohibited until 1788. The real efficiency of the system, however, had ceased long before. Even in the late years of the seventeenth century negro slaves were more in demand for supplying old plantations or beginning new ones than servants, and where a demand existed for white servants it was for artisans and apprentices, and large prices had to be paid to get good ones.[2] White servitude survived after the downfall of the system in an apprenticeship of domestic growth, originating in the binding of poor or bastard children for a term of years for their instruction and to save the parish the expense of their support; but this had no historic connection with the apprenticeship which constituted a part of indented servitude, and itself finally passed away under the regime of perfectly free labor.

The experience of Virginia was largely repeated in the other colonies, and the general effects of the system were

sembly to discourage the slave trade. (Hening, I., 540; III., 193, 213, 225, 229, 233; Tucker's Blackstone, I., Appd., 51; Minor, Inst., I., 164). The importation of negroes, however, could not be checked, and the chief advantage Virginia reaped from these acts was a large revenue for her public works. In 1705 the number of 1800 negroes was brought in, and in 1708 there were 12,000 negro tithables compared with 18,000 white, while the revenue from white servants was too inconsiderable to deserve notice. (Va. MS. B. R. O., Nov. 27, 1708, Jennings to Lds. of Trade.) Intended insurrections of negroes in 1710, 1722, 1730, bear witness to their alarming increase, and by the middle of the century the blacks were almost as numerous as the whites. Va. MSS. B. R. O., V., pt. 2, p. 352; II., pt. I., 211; 1708, Nov. 21; 1710, June 10; 1712, July 26; 1722, Dec. 22; Burke, 210; Cal. Va. State Papers, I, 129, 130.

[1] Ford's Washington, II., 408, note.

[2] Fitzhugh, Letters, Jan. 30, 1686-87, 1686, Aug. 15, 1690; Wm. Byrd's Letters, Feb. 25, 1683, June 21, 1864, Mar. 29, 1685, 1686, May, June, Nov.

I

much the same in all. The influence on internal development was even more clearly marked in Maryland and Pennsylvania than in Virginia. In Pennsylvania the large number of German settlers who came in this way, driven from
home by religious or political persecution, became the most
valued of citizens.[1] The rise and influence of the freedman
in Maryland was as perceptible as in Virginia. Though
that colony was unfortunate in receiving a larger number of
the convict class, very few of them seem to have remained
in the country on attaining their freedom, but returned to
Europe or migrated to distant settlements.[2] In the other
southern and middle colonies and in New England servants
were not numerically so large a class, and their rise and absorption into the higher classes became from social and
political reasons even more easy than in Virginia and Maryland.[3]

The actual conditions of servitude varied somewhat in the
different colonies, assuming in some respects a harsher, in
others a milder character than we have seen in Virginia.
Thus in Massachusetts the elective franchise seems to have
been exercised by servants only up to the year 1636, and the
qualification of church membership was required of all voters
to 1664. In Virginia the " inhabitants " voted for burgesses
until 1646, and until 1670 the freed servant enjoyed the suffrage along with other free men, there being no property
or other qualification.[4] The terms of servitude also in many

[1] Kalm, Travels, I., 29, 388, 390. They were frequently in good
circumstances, and sold themselves to learn the language or
methods of agriculture.

[2] Gambrall's Colonial Life of Maryland, 165, and Neill's Found-
ers, 77, quoted in Brackett, Negro in Md.; Eddis, Letters, 63, 66,
67.

[3] Plymouth Col. Laws, VIII., pt. III., 34, 35, 47, 58, 61, 65, 81,
140, 195.

[4] Hurd, I., 254 sq.; Bancroft, I., 322; Conn. Rev. S., 40; Hening,
I., 300, 334, 403, 411, 475; II., 82, 280, 356, 380; Col. Rec. Va.
Assemb., 1619. Hurd, I., pp. 228-311, gives a valuable abstract
of all laws relating to bondage in the colonies.

of the colonies were longer than in Virginia. In Maryland the common term seems to have been five years. Seven-
year terms were frequent in Massachusetts, and in Rhode
Island even ten. Provision was taken for the strict enforcement of the full term, and enfranchisement was not encouraged. Additions of time, corporal punishment, limitation of the rights of trade and free marriage, and provisions
for the capture and return of runaways, were much the same.[1]
Greater numbers of Indian and mulatto servants seem to
have been made use of in New England than in the other
colonies, though the importation of white servants was specially encouraged by the enactments against Indian slave-trad-
ing. Georgia and the Carolinas also encouraged the importation of servants of the better class, while the colonies in
general made an attempt to protect themselves against convicts and servants of undesirable classes, as Irish Papists and
aliens.[2]

The wide prevalence of the system, not only in the American but in the island plantations of England, had a most
important bearing on the social economy of Great Britain
and of other European countries, similar in a less degree to
the effect of the large European emigration of the present
day. Not only were many of the evils of a congested population lessened, but elements of the greatest social and political danger were effectively gotten rid of by forced transportation.[3] The effect on England of the removal of large num-

---

[1] Eddis, 63; Hurd, I., 271 sq., 309, 310; Pa. Laws, 1700-1, 13 sq.,
230, 552.

[2] Hurd, I., 271 sq.

[3] 4 Geo., c. 11; 6 Geo. III., c. 32; 8 Geo. III., c. 15; 19 Geo. III., c.
14; Prendergast, 52, 53, 163, note; Carlyle's Cromwell, II., 457;
Neill, Va. Vet., 102, 103. As the Stuarts systematically encouraged
the deportation of troublesome persons and petty criminals to
the American colonies, so Oliver Cromwell in preparing for his
settlement of Ireland did not hesitate to transport large numbers of the dispossessed Irish as slaves to the West Indies,
or as servants to the English plantations in America, nor to
sell the survivors of the Drogheda massacre as slaves to
Barbadoes. Until stopped by the War of the Revolution, the

bers of political and social offenders was wholly beneficial; and though many of the emigrants from the Continent were religious or political refugees, a great number were also from the poorer classes, and their withdrawal was a considerable economic relief.

In conclusion an important political effect on the American colonies should be noted. The infusion of such large numbers of the lower and middle classes into colonial society could only result in a marked increase of democratic sentiment, which, together with a spirit of rebellion against the unjust importation of convicts and slaves, increased under British tyranny the growing restlessness which finally led to the separation of the colonies from the mother country.[1]

---

penal statutes of the Georges continued to send the felons of Scotland and England to the American colonies. (Cf. DeFoe, " Moll Flanders " (1686) and " Captain Jack.") Large numbers of servants were brought into Maryland and Pennsylvania from Germany, Switzerland and Holland. They were generally known as " Redemptioners," from redeeming their persons from the power of the shipmaster who transported them, usually by a voluntary sale into servitude. The system continued in active operation in Maryland well up to the year 1819. Cf. Laws, Feb. 16, 1818.

[1] Franklin, Works (Bigelow ed.), IV., 108, 254. Jefferson, Works (Ford ed.), II., 11, 52, 53.

BIBLIOGRAPHY.

Anburey, T. Travels through America, 1776-81. 2 vols. London, 1789.

Anson, Sir Wm. R. The Principles of the English Law of Contract. 3d ed. Oxford, 1884.

Ashley, W. J. Introduction to English Economic History and Theory. 2d ed. London, 1893. 12mo.

Bacon, Sir Francis. Essays. 8vo. Boston, 1868.

Bancroft, George. History of the United States of America. 6 vols. 8vo. Rev. ed. N. Y. 1883.

Beverley, Robert. History of Virginia. Reprint from 2d London ed. Richmond, 1855.

Blackstone, Sir Wm. Commentaries on the Laws of England. 4 vols. N. Y. 1859-62.

Brackett, J. R. Negro in Maryland. J. H. U. Studies. Extra vol. VI. Baltimore, 1889.

Brown, Alexander. The Genesis of the United States, 1605-1616. 2 vols. Boston, 1890.

Bruce, John. Annals of the Honorable East India Company, 1600-1707-8. 3 vols. 4to. London, 1810.

Burk, John Daly. History of Virginia. 4 vols. 8vo. Petersburg, 1804-16.

Burke, Edmund. European Settlements in America. 2d ed. 2 vols. 8vo. London, 1758.

Byrd, Col. Wm. History of the Dividing Line and other Tracts (Westover MSS., vol. II.). Richmond, 1866. MS. Letters of, (1683-91). Va. Hist. Soc., Richmond, Va.

Calendar of English State Papers. Colonial Series, 1513-1676. 6 vols. 8vo. Ed. by W. Noel Sainsbury. London, 1860, 1862, 1880. Domestic Series, 1581-1625, 1649-56, 1660-67. 27 vols. Ed. by Mary A. E. Green. 1625-41. 17 vols. Ed. by Jno. Bruce and W. D. Hamilton.

Calendar of Virginia State Papers and other MSS., 1652-1793, preserved in the Capitol at Richmond. Ed. by Wm. P. Palmer. 6 vols. 4to. Richmond, 1875-86.

Campbell, Charles. History of the Colony and Dominion of Virginia. (Lippincott) Philadelphia, 1860.

Chalmers, George. Political Annals of the Present United Colonies. 4 vols. London, 1780.

Cooke, John Esten. Virginia, a History of the People. Boston, 1884.

Cunningham, Wm. Growth of English Industry and Commerce in Modern Times. 8vo. Cambridge, 1892.

I

Bibliography. 97

De Jarnette. MSS. relating to the Early History of Virginia,
preserved in the State Capitol, Richmond. 2 vols. folio.

Doyle, J. A. English Colonies in America. 3 vols. N. Y. 1882.

Essex County Records, MS., 1683-86. (State Library, Richmond,
Va.)

Eddis, Wm. Letters from America, historical and descriptive,
1769-77. London, 1792. 8vo.

Fitzhugh, Wm. MS. Letters of, 1679-99. Va. Hist. Soc., Richmond, Va.

Force, Peter. Tracts and other Papers relating to the Colonies
in North America. 4 vols. 8vo. Washington, 1836-46.

Franklin, Benjamin. Works; edited by J. B. Bigelow. 10 vols.
N. Y. 1887.

Fyffe, C. A. History of Modern Europe. 3 vols. 8vo. N. Y.
1886-89.

General Court of Virginia. MS. Records of, 1670-76. 1 v. folio.
(Va. Hist. Soc., Richmond, Va.)

Hakluyt, Richard. Collection of Early Voyages, Travels and
Discoveries of the English Nation. 5 v. 4to. London, 1809-
12.

Hening, Wm. Waller. Statutes at Large of Virginia. 13 v. 8vo.
Richmond, 1812. The New Virginia Justice. Richmond, 1799.

Henrico County Records, MS., 1686-99. 4 v. folio. (State Library, Richmond, Va.)

Howe, Henry. Historical Collections of Virginia. Charleston,
S. C., 1852.

Hotten, J. C. Original Lists of Emigrants, 1600-1700. London,
1874.

Hurd, John C., LL. D. The Law of Freedom and Bondage in
the United States. 2 v. 8vo. Boston, 1858-62.

Jefferson, Thomas. MSS. of, 1606-1711. 7 v. fo. Letters, Patents, Proclamations, Correspondence, 1622, 1623, 1625; Orders,
1622-27, and Instructions to Governors; Council Book, 1679-
1700; Laws, 1623-1711, with some omissions. Library of Congress, Law Dept., under title, cap. 19, 226; cap. 23, 199, 217,
218, 220, 221. Six vols. are largely contained in Hening and
Burk. Writings; ed. H. A. Washington. 9 v. 8vo. N. Y.
1859. Writings; ed. P. L. Ford. 4 v. N. Y. 1892. Reports
of Cases, General Ct. of Va., 1730-1740 and 1768-1792. 8vo.
Charlottesville, 1829.

Jones, Rev. Hugh. Present State of Virginia. (Sabin, J., Reprints.) 8vo. N. Y. 1865.

Kalm, Peter. Travels into North America. 3 v. 8vo. London,
1771.

Land books of Virginia. MS., 1621—. Land Office in the Capitol
at Richmond.

Lecky, W. E. H. History of England in the 18th Century. 8 v.
8vo. London, 1878-82.

Lodge, Henry Cabot. A Short History of the English Colonies.
Rev. ed. N. Y. 1881.

MacDonald, Col. Angus M. MSS. relating to the Early History of Virginia. 2 v. fo. (State Library, Richmond, Va.)

Madison, James. Papers of; ed. by H. D. Gilpin. 3 v. 8vo. N. Y. 1844.

Massachusetts Historical Society Collections. 4th Series. 6 v. 8vo. Boston, 1852-65.

Middlesex Co., England, Records. 4 v. 1888. Ed. by J. C. Jeaffreson.

Minor, John B., LL. D. Institutes of Common and Statute Law. 4 v. Richmond.

Neill, E. D. History of the Virginia Company of London (1606-24). 4to. Albany, 1869. Virginia Carolorum (1625-85). Albany, 1869. The English Colonization of America. London, 1871. Virginia Vetusta, 1885.

Northampton (Accomac) County Records, MS. 2 v. folio. (State Library, Richmond, Va.) 1632—.

Oldmixon, John. British Empire in America. 2 v. 12mo. London, 1708.

Pennsylvania, Genl. Assembly Acts, 1700-97. 4 v.

Prendergast, J. P. The Cromwellian Settlement in Ireland. London, 1865.

Purchas, Samuel. His Pilgrimes. 5 v. fo. London, 1625-26.

Reeves, J. History of the English Law. 5 v. (Finlason Ed.) 1880.

Richmond Standard. Richmond, Va. 1880.

Royal Commission on Historical Manuscripts, Reports of the. 8 v. London, 1870-81.

Smith, Capt. John. General History. 2 v. 8vo. Richmond, 1819. Works, 1608-31; ed. by Arber. 1 v. 8vo. Birmingham, 1884.

Spottswood, Gov. Alexander. Official Letters of. 2 v. Va. Hist. Coll., N. S., ed. by R. A. Brock, 1882.

Statutes at Large of England and Great Britain. 20 v. London, 1811.

Statutes at Large of Virginia, 1792—.

Stevens, Henry. Dawn of British Trade (Court Minutes of the East India Co., 1599-1603). 8vo. London, 1886.

Stith, Wm. History of the Discovery and Settlement of Virginia to 1624. (Sabin, J., Reprints.) N. Y. 1865.

Strachey, W. Historie of Travaile into Virginia Britannia. Ed. by Major. Hakluyt Society. Vol. 6. 1849. Lawes Divine, Morall and Martial, 1612—. (Force, vol. III.)

Surtees Society, Publications of the. 84 v. 8vo. London, 1835-89.

Taswell-Langmead, T. P. English Constitutional History. 4th ed. London, 1890.

Thurloe, John. Collections of State Papers; ed. by T. Birch. 7 v. London, 1742.

Tucker, St. George. Commentaries on Blackstone. 2 v. Richmond.

Verney Family Papers; ed. by J. Bruce. No. 56 Camden Soc. Pub., 1866.

Virginia, Colonial Records of (1619-80). State Senate Doc. 4to.

——Declaration of the State of the Colony of. London, 1620.

——New Description of, 1649. (Force, II.)

——Historical Magazine. 2 v. Ed. by P. A. Bruce. Richmond, 1893-4.

——Historical Register; ed. by Wm. Maxwell. 6 v. Richmond, 1848.

——Historical Society, Collections of. 10 v. Ed. by R. A. Brock. Richmond, 1882-91.

——Present State, 1696. Blair, Chilton & Hartwell. London, 1727.

Virginia Company, MS. Records of the. (a) Collingwood MS. 2 v. fo. v. I. April 28, 1619-May 8, 1622; v. II. May 20, 1622-June 7, 1624. (b) Randolph MS. 2 v. fo. *Ibid.* 1 v. fo. Miscellaneous (1617—).

Washington, George. Writings of. Ed. by W. C. Ford. 9 v. N. Y. 1889.

——*Ibid.* Ed. by Jared Sparks. 12 v. Boston.

Whitaker, Alexander. Good Newes from Virginia. London, 1613.

Williams, E. Virginia Truly Valued. London, 1650.

Winder MS. 2 v. fo. 1606-76. (State Library, Richmond, Va.)

Wirt, William. Life of Patrick Henry. Philadelphia, 1817.

——The Letters of the British Spy. N. Y. 1832.

York County Records, MS., 1633-1709. 10 v. fo. State Library, Richmond, Va.

I

INDEX

.

www.ingramcontent.com/pod-product-compliance
Lightning Source LLC
LaVergne TN
LVHW021611080426
835510LV00019B/2520

9 780788 417078